THE IMPORT BIBLE
(2019 Edition)

THE COMPLETE BEGINNER'S
GUIDE TO SUCCESSFUL
IMPORTING FROM CHINA

First edition: March 2015
Updated version 20.01.2019

TABLE OF CONTENTS:

PART 2: The Import Bible – Professional Edition..... 117

PART 1
THE IMPORT BIBLE – BEGINNERS GUIDE

CHAPTER 1
ABOUT THE AUTHOR:

My name is Manuel and I was born in Austria in a little town called Melk. Asia has always fascinated me, ever since I can remember. I remember watching Bruce Lee and other Chinese movies as a kid and I was hooked right away.

My professional career started in 1998 when I worked for Austria's biggest DIY retailer (bauMax www.baumax.at). I moved to Hong Kong in 2005 when I was offered a position as an intern at one of the biggest sourcing offices in Hong Kong, with a staff over 200 people.

For more than 10 years I worked with the biggest retailers in the world, developing, sourcing, and finding new products for them. These retailers included: Metro, Rewe, OBI, Carrefour, Tesco, Wal-Mart, Amazon, Auchan, Lowes, Sears, Home Depot and many others.

As you can imagine, the big retailers expect their products to do more than just conform to standards and regulations when they purchase them in Asia. They need to be of the highest standard and quality. These retailers cannot afford to have a product recalled due to quality problems or defective components. These products need to be top-notch.

In those 10 years I got to know all about the standards and product requirements, and additionally I gained a lot of experience and insight working with factories in China.

Not just that. I learned a lot about China, its culture, and its manufacturing facilities: where and how to find the best suppliers, how to negotiate and communicate with them, how to arrange business travel for my customers, and a lot more.

In the busiest seasons (April and October), I accompanied up to 30 buyers a month to exhibitions, factories and showrooms to help negotiate, develop products and follow up on the buyer's requests after they were gone. I got to know all the tips and tricks you need to return home from your trip successfully.

This eBook is aimed to make you a professional importer in a few days, using what took me over 10 years to learn.

This eBook will guide you step-by-step on the process of importing goods from China.

This eBook aims to take away all your worries and doubts and help you to take your business to the next level!

I will cover all aspects of importing from China. Starting with several online supplier sourcing sites such as Globalsources.com and Alibaba.com, you'll get to know about importing procedures, dealing with factories, finding your products, how to inspect and ship your goods, and finding out what legal import requirements your products need. In Part 3 I cover **taking your business to an even higher level when going to China,** including: travel arrangements, visas, customs clearance, how to negotiate with suppliers in factories, tips and tricks to get you the best prices, and simple etiquette in China.

I've updated this eBook in January 2019 to reflect changes in the industry as well as insights learned since first publishing this eBook.

Where am I now? I've spoken at large conferences around the world on importing, exporting, Amazon FBA and ecommerce in general. I now run several online and ecommerce businesses as well as coaching programs that teach importing from China here: http://importdojo.com

I also run a personal blog and site over at: www.manuelbecvar.com

On this page I document my entrepreneurial journey as well as making money online. If you sign up on this site you'll also receive my FREE 200+ pages eBook on making money online.

If you have any questions feel free to email me at: info@manuelbecvar.com

I also invite you to join my FREE Facebook groups where like-minded entrepreneurs share their ideas, thoughts and process:

Facebook group for making money online and entrepreneurial things: https://www.facebook.com/groups/504810863347354/

Facebook group for importing from China and Amazon FBA: https://www.facebook.com/groups/1585493201714528/?ref=br_rs

CHAPTER 2
HOW IT ALL STARTED AND WHAT THIS E-BOOK IS ABOUT

When I started my own company in late 2013 my goal was to provide affordable consumer electronics to customers that don't have a buying office in Asia and customers that do not import by themselves.

Before I started my own company I was working with large retailers and they all had their import processes in place. But my target customers with my own company were not these retailers. My target customers were people with small businesses or online shops and wholesalers that would like to get things directly from the source at a great price.

In the first few months I felt that many of my new customers were uneducated or unaware about importing procedures and many didn't know the advantages and disadvantages. So instead of explaining everything in detail in every email I decided to make a guide that they could use every day. What started out as a few pages quickly turned into a book. To be exact it's the book that you are reading today - the **Import Bible**.

I have helped many customers and buyers all over the world with this e-book and many tell me that this information has helped them a great deal to take their business to the next level.

For example, I had a customer from Spain. He was selling small quantities of product that he bought from importers in Spain with little profit on Ebay. He was looking for a way to grow his business but had no idea about the import process. When I started to work with him in March 2014 he had a total profit of 800EUR a month through his eBay sales. As of today, because of my help, he is one of the top-sellers on eBay with a profit of over 50,000EUROS and now selling on Amazon with a turnover of 60,000USD within the first 4 months.

I will show you how to turn an investment of 10,000USD into **33,000USD PROFIT!**

With this book I want to help you to have the same success as he did with just a couple of months of hard work. Yes, hard work. Don't let the title of this book fool you. To take your ideas or business a step forward takes a lot of hard work. This book is also a great tool for you as a general guide and introduction to importing.

There are a few chapters that may not apply to you. I recommend reading them anyway and then deciding for yourself whether to apply these processes or not.

I hope you enjoy reading this book and I hope it will help you the same way it has helped many others.

Enjoy,
Manuel

CHAPTER 3
ABOUT CHINA

There are a lot of statistics I could give you but I wouldn't know where to begin.

I want to break down China and its manufacturing in a few sentences.

Believe it or not, China is still the biggest production site by far. While there are several countries in the vicinity, such as Vietnam, Thailand, and Bangladesh, they simply do not have the infrastructure that China does.

Imagine you need sanitary items, furniture, household appliances, insurance, and a smart phone. You walk into a Wal-Mart. You can find practically anything you need in there and that's within 10,000 square feet. That pretty much sums up China's infrastructure.

Factory A provides plastic and tooling, Factory B provides packaging, Factory C provides raw material and components, and Factory D assembles everything. They are all within a stone's throw away from each other. Most of the factory bosses are related to each other. They set up a perfect system within their "community."

I'll give you an example, and I am not kidding you, 95% of the world's supply of electrical multi-sockets comes from a small town in Cixi near Ningbo/Shanghai. When I say "small" I actually mean small for China. There are over 1.4 million people in this town.

When you step into "Ningbo Kaifeng" (the largest factory in the world for multi-sockets) you are overwhelmed. And when you step outside of the building you see five competitors across the street. All the factory bosses are related to each other. And down the street they can find everything they need – factories that make packaging, tooling, plastic, steel, and so on.

The Chinese are so effective in terms of production and infrastructure that some first world countries could really learn a lot.

The big retailers figured out a long time ago that nearly every large corporation, retailer, discounter, or online shop has a buying office somewhere in China/Hong Kong. I know this because I have been in the industry for over 15 years. When you walk into a factory and look at the production line you see cartons of goods with famous names on them. Whether it is a fan from Home Depot, an audio speaker from Target, or a ceramic pot from Bed, Bath, & Beyond, they were all made in China.

Most products are made in specific areas.

Here are a few examples:

- **Guangdong province** (South of China): Electronics of any kind, especially consumer and household, toys
- **Zhejiang province** (Shanghai area): DIY products, tools, metal and fabrics, lighting
- **Hebei province** (Beijing area): Textiles, coal, steel, iron, engineering, chemicals, power, ceramics and food

These are the main areas for production. However, nowadays production is also shifting inland to take advantage of lower labor and production costs.

And that's why China will be Number 1 for production and export for many years to come.

CHAPTER 4
WHY SHOULD YOU IMPORT?

I would generally say there are two main reasons why you should import yourself.

1) There is a saying. **"Margin is made in purchasing, not selling."**

Every successful buyer in the world who works for a larger company will tell you that it's all about the purchasing. Profits are made when buying and not selling.

Huh? Yes sure, there is a profit to be made in selling but what if you are not the only one selling this product? Then you have to work for your margin at the root and not when selling the product. The competition doesn't sleep – they spend their time doing research on you and your sales price. If they match or even lower their price you have a problem. You have to decide if you want to accept a loss in margin or look for a new supplier. And you don't want to go to your importer for that. You go to the source directly, and that's the factory in China. This is the **1ˢᵗ part** of the book.

2) Apart from reason No.1 there is also the **"innovator effect"** to be taken in account. Say your competitor buys the same or a similar product to what you have and probably from the same source (your importer). You don't want that. You want to have a great product with a great margin but you want it to be sold in your shop/store only. So **you have to be the first one who finds it** and make a deal with the manufacturer to have it exclusively. And the only way this is done is

by visiting China and going to factories to see their products, and perhaps even developing your own product or private label.

Here are some more reasons for you to consider importing from China:

Advantages

- Low manufacturing costs
- Suppliers are much more open to working with smaller businesses and providing smaller quantities
- Large number of suppliers to choose from
- For many products, China might be the only place that produces the item
- One-stop services like Globalsources have made it very easy to navigate and purchase from suppliers

Along with the advantages of sourcing from overseas suppliers also come several disadvantages that you should be equally aware of. Some of the biggest disadvantages include:

Disadvantages

- Perceived lower quality of items
- (Usually) lower manufacturing and labor standards
- Almost no intellectual property protection
- Language and communication barriers can be difficult to overcome
- Difficult/costly to visit manufacturer on-site
- Longer shipping time
- Cultural differences in business practices
- Product importation and customs clearance

- Lower level of payment security and less recourse if something goes wrong

HOWEVER, with this eBook I will take away these fears and disadvantages and prepare you for a trouble-free import.

CHAPTER 5
THE 6-STEP IMPORT PROCESS

This is a rather large section so I will outline the six steps and go into detail in later chapters.

The 6-step import process

This is the general outline of the process. We will look into each process in greater detail in later sections. It is also the same process whether you go to China or sit in the comfort of your home.

These are the **6 steps** that you always need to follow through no matter what product you want to import.

1) Decide where your product will be manufactured. In our case this will be China or South East Asia (depending on the product).

Countries have different export/import regulations. While products may be cheap to buy from Asia, there are many other factors that might add costs. Requirements for importing specific commodities depend on a wide variety of criteria. Some information, such as whether an item is subject to quota restrictions, eligible for reduced rates of duty, or restricted from entry because it originates in an embargoed country, can be determined only if you know the item's Harmonized Tariff customs number. This can be found for the US, for example, under: http://hts.usitc.gov/.

If you live in Europe or any other country simply Google "customs tariff number **your country**."

Click on the link and head over to the country's official government website.

On these databases you can simply look for a product's tariff or regulation information.

You can also try https://simplyduty.com , a site that gives you five free chances to look up information. The rest is premium and paid services. It's a great way to find out all the costs of taxes and customs fees you have to consider.

At these sites you will also find a lot of tips on items that have "anti-dumping" tax on them to minimize the import and protect the local industry.

2) Find a product

You may want to have a niche product or an item where you can make large profits. We will go into this in more detail later.

3) Find a supplier

This is the most exciting but also the most difficult part. We go into this in greater detail later. If you are new to importing there is usually a lot of support from your local government, which is ready to answer your questions. But the purpose of this e-book is to help you to understand **the process by yourself.**

4) Calculate all duties and taxes

This goes hand-in-hand with the first part of the process. Import duties can be calculated in different ways and can make or break your business.

I have a rule of thumb: I take the buying price from my supplier and add 20-30% on top. This gives me a rough idea of what my landing price will be. This rule applies to first-world places like the US, Europe, Canada, Hong Kong, and Singapore, for example. Many second or third world countries are not so open to importing and put a high percentage of duties and tax on top of import products to protect the local industry. Many first world countries have 0% duties and tax to encourage imports.

This applies especially to "green products" that are very sustainable and help reduce energy or waste. A good example is an LED bulb with 0% tax and duties. Of course, you can check for more information using Customs Tariff Numbers (see above) or resources like www.simplyduty.com

We will go through an example in Chapter 19: Calculate your costs.

5) Find a freight forwarder and customs broker

Don't do this process (logistics) yourself. It can be a nightmare, trust me. Ask your supplier, who usually has his own forwarders, to give you contacts. If you already have contacts in the industry, great. If not, we will also provide you with a list of freight forwarders and customs brokers. The freight forwarder usually knows all the procedures and documents that are necessary. This rule applies to bulk shipments in containers only. If you only have a few samples or pieces to be sent then use airmail or couriers such as DHL/TNT/FEDEX. We will also give you some contacts in this course. Oftentimes your supplier has a preferred courier for samples with great rates. Ask him to provide them to you.

6) Monitor your shipment and have an inspection!

If you are having a larger shipment or products that are valuable you **NEED** to hire a third-party for inspection. This third-party can inspect your shipment during or after production and send you a report. Based on this report you can give the supplier the release of the shipment or have him **REWORK** your goods. If there are problems found during your inspection the supplier will **ALWAYS agree** to rework your shipment because he is still waiting for the rest of his money, which you will only release to him once you are happy with your shipment (**do not pay** 100% of your order up-front, **EVER**).

Many importers skip this step to save costs or trust their suppliers completely. **TRUST ME**, in my 10 years working with factories for my buyers I could tell you tons of stories where the products were not 100% according to my order requirements. It could be a wrong instruction manual, many scratches on the product, a faulty wire, or heavily damaged carton boxes. Don't let me discourage you – many times it's just minor mistakes that can be accepted, but, again, since I worked for the biggest retailers in the world, products needed to be top-notch. Once you let your supplier know that you will do an inspection on your products he is more likely to pay more attention to your order too. And the best part? This can be done for ~300USD from companies like Asia-Inspection (my favourite & most competitive prices inspection company), TUV, Bureau Veritas, and many more.

CHAPTER 6
HOW TO FIND THE RIGHT PRODUCT

As mentioned earlier this can be a very lengthy process or a very short one if you already have something in mind. I will give you a few ideas and guidelines if you don't have a new product idea yet.

Unfortunately, China's factories rely a lot on your product input. Most of the time you can also request a little modification such as putting your company logo on the item, private label packaging, or changing the colors of the product.

We will cover custom products in the section OEM Products.

Other than that you will need to rely on factories for their input.

What you can give them without investing a lot of money for new products (that no one has yet) is a good pitch. Say you see some new cool gadget on websites like Engadget", Wired, CNet, PCMag (to name a few in the technology sector). You could send this idea to your trusted supplier and ask them if they would be willing to invest in developing this product. Or perhaps he has something very similar already in his assortment.

Fortunately, what Chinese factories are very good at is producing standard items that you can find in your local Wal-Mart / Sears / Lowes / Bed, Bath, & Beyond, and many more. These items can be a bathroom accessory, TVs, garden furniture, and much more.

One of the best ways for me to find a new product is by **scouting the Internet** and looking at trendy websites.

For example, this link provides all the necessary company websites that you need: http://www.kadaza.com/.

Just click on any category and browse through the many major websites provided.

For example, click on "Computer & Tech" and you will find the top 24 websites where you can start your research on the product that you would like to import. It is time consuming but it's also a great way to find ideas and scout your potential competitors.

What also helps me a lot are **newsletters**. I subscribe to at least 100 newsletters of companies that I think provide cool gadgets and items. This way you get weekly newsletters of trending products. Simply go onto a company's website and subscribe, easy as that. It could be your local supermarket, a big brand name company, or some blog that always features the coolest and trendiest items. Perhaps you could **create a new email address** that you register with on these sites so that your main (work) email address doesn't get overwhelmed with newsletters.

Another way to find new products is obviously when you are **out in a shopping mall**. To start your own import business means that you also work when you are out with friends/family at a shopping mall. Keep your eyes open and when you see something cool make a reminder for yourself on your smart phone to look up this product.

Travelling is also a great way to find ideas. When you are out of your country or state you will likely see items that your country/state does not have. There could be many reasons why they may not be available where you live, but it's always worth it to check an idea out. I remember when my friend told me about 10 years ago about Bubble

Tea & Fancy Green Tea drinks sold in Hong Kong and Asia. She was from Germany and she had never seen these drinks back home. She didn't go on any further with that idea but a few years later back in Germany these drinks started to pop up and were a smashing hit! So even when you think at first that idea might be nothing, it could be worth millions! Share the idea with a few friends and brainstorm about it.

One of my favorite and an efficient way to find new products is at **exhibitions**.

There are hundreds of exhibitions each year in many countries. You get to meet the supplier, see the products, and talk over details such as prices, models, and much more. On top of all of that I guarantee you that you will get inspired. To find exhibitions near you just Google the exhibition center near you and get your entry ticket. Most times you will need to provide name cards and contact details for that. You can order business cards for $5 these days. Going to an exhibition prepared and with a professional image gives the supplier a great impression of you. I will cover exhibitions and how to behave there in another chapter in my next book.

Obviously, looking at **competitors** can help you find a product. But doing so means you need to be more price competitive and that gives you a disadvantage, unless you are selling at a different price level and providing additional services that your customers value.

Amazon, Ebay, and the likes can help you get started on basic product ideas. I don't recommend starting by importing products that the majority of companies already have. But these websites give you great input on trends and items that sell very well.

Alibaba, Aliexpress, Global Sources, and Taobao are great ways to find products. You could search through millions of products from thousands of suppliers. But I don't recommend this option, as you can quickly get lost in the products. These sites are a great way to find a supplier, however. We will cover these four sources later.

Now, having said all that, you might think, "but how do I figure out what product is right for me?" Again, all options above give you some ideas where to find products, but it is up to you to try and test them. You can start by importing small quantities via **Aliexpress (dropshipping)** and testing them through your EbayEbay/Amazon or other sales channels.

Make sure that the product you want to import is not regulated or a restricted item in your country. Do your research! See the section The 6 Step Import Process.

To make this easier for you I am going to run you through an example:

How to find a product?

This is the number 1 question I get asked on almost a daily basis. I have no definite answer for you today but I will try to break it down in two sections and a step by step guide on how I select products and hopefully you'll get a few ideas

Lets look at your personal situation (scenario) first and then see how you can benefit from your scenario when picking the product.

1) How to pick your product niche:

Scenario 1: You've got money

Congratulations! While it is easier to get started the question of what product you are going to pick still remains open. More on that below.

Scenario 2: You don't have money and you're scraping together every little cent you have to reach 5,000$ because that's the budget you heard of is the minimum (well its my minimum that I recommend to everyone).

While it is more difficult to get started you have the same starting point like everyone else out there. You probably want to make sure that the product you are going to pick is worth the investment. But even if your first product is not a killer don't worry. You learn a lot in the process and in most cases you can at least get your investment back. Read on.

Scenario 3: You have a large follower-ship on social media

You are in a great spot. You already have a list of customers to get your launch and product going. It is imperative to pick a product that fits your social media.

In my recent case study (https://importdojo.com/case-study-how-i-went-from-zero-to-7000us-in-10-days-in-one-of-the-most-competitive-amazon-niches/) I reached out to bloggers and that boosted my launch immensely. Even nearly 3 months after my launch I still get sales from that site.

What does that mean if you have a large followership? Lets say I have an Instagram account with 50,000 followers that talks about eating healthy, fitness, the outdoors etc. I could launch so many products to that followership, even competitive niches. For example:

- Yoga mats
- Accessories for the gym (tumblers, bags, sporting items etc.)
- Backpacks, travelling gear, camping accessories
- etc.

When you research your future niche and have decided on it build social media right away if possible. A client of mine built a social media follower-ship of 8,000 followers within 2 months (various social sites) and then launched her product. She sold nearly 100 pieces the first week only trough social media. That helped boost her organic sales and the rest is history.

So consider social media right from the beginning when choosing a product.

Ideally you will want to enlarge your assortment with similar products that all fit into your following. For example if your first product was a yoga mat and your followership is about exercising etc. it probably doesn't make a lot of sense that your next product is a vacuum cleaner.

Scenario 4: You have passion about a certain product category

Let's just say you love the outdoors, hiking, camping, and exercising in general (like me). So many products to choose from but you have one advantage. You know what you like and what your product should be able to do. You already have an advantage over many other competitors. Your passion for this category goes into your product. E.g. if you were to be upset about quality of camping mats you would already know what to tell your supplier where to improve. Look into categories you have passion for and then choose a product that you feel you can talk about, improve and passion in selling for.

For example if you like cooking you could look at developing a product that makes a certain cooking process easier. The exciting thing about this is that all your passion also goes into your product and listing and people just buy your stuff because you are so convinced of your product yourself.

For example I recently bought a travel bag from a German entrepreneur based in Thailand who loves travelling. Over the years he went trough so many of his traveling bags already because they were of poor quality (the straps broke, the leather peeled off etc.) and he decided to make his own bags. After 6 months of hard work he launched his site and product and it took off immediately. All his passion went into his product and site (https://www.travlmind.com/). You could tell by his story that he was really passionate about creating the best bags out there and not just copying the big brands. And only that convinced me to buy one of the bags even that it was at a higher price tag.

Scenario 5: You have vast experience in a certain industry

Lets imagine you have 17 years of experience in selling electronics (like me). What was the first product I picked? It was an electronic item. Why? Because that's where I had my experience in. I believe you should not just have passion about your product but also have experience. When I sell a product online I want to be able to answer customers questions and inquires. To be able to do that I need experience in that category. Your passion and experience goes into creating your product.

So when I choose my first product I improved an existing item based on my experience in that industry: https://importdojo.com/how-i-started-my-own-private-label/

So if you have a lot of experience in a certain industry make that industry your first product category. Don't have experience in a certain industry? What about a hobby? Or are you a parent? I am sure if you are a parent you have lots of experience with your kid/children and you could start in that category

Scenario 6: You have none of the above

Not to worry or be frustrated. Most of the people I know that get started start with Scenario 6 and there are still many success stories out there if you are within this scenario. Here's an approach that you could use:

First: Take out a notebook and create a list of your interests and hobbies (or responsibilities as a parent for example) e.g. kitchen products, electronics, sports, your kids etc.. Yes actually write it down. Call me a bit old fashioned but I like to drop down ideas in written

Second: subscribe to newsletters of companies that talk about or sell products of your interests. See below on which sites for example (point 2)

Third: Gather a list of potential products from that niche. Collect at least 10 ideas.

Fourth: Research phase. Junglescout, Amazon, eBay, jet.com, **local shop that sells the products** etc.
See if there is any demand? Or is there space for one more seller (you)?

Fifth: If there is no demand is it because the product is in its fledging stages? Can you improve the product with your passion and interest in this product? Yes? Create a To-Do list of what you can improve based on customers reviews, what friends and family say etc. and move onto finding a supplier.

Sixth: No? Are you still convinced of the product? Follow your gut feeling and also ask around in friend circles. Move onto finding a supplier

Seven: No demand at all? Move onto product 2 of your list of ideas.

Lets say you found your niche, category or general product idea. Depending on above scenarios here are a few examples on how to find your product:

2) How to find your product ideas:

Choose your scenario and lets look at the following options:

1. Amazon
2. Blogs, Gadget or trendy sites
3. Exhibitions
4. Supermarkets, shopping malls
5. Tools
6. When travelling
7. Alibaba & Globalsources

1) Amazon

You could look for hours on Amazon in the different categories and niches if you already have a certain product idea. But if you have no idea to start I suggest you start with the best seller list: http://amzn.to/1ZN3rY3

2) Blogs, gadget or trendy sites

Please don't just look on Amazon! While there are great tools out there to scout Amazon for products (Junglescout, Cashcowpro etc.) I get many of my ideas outside Amazon.

One of my favorite site to find interesting blogs and trendy websites is Kadaza. It's a collection of the best and most interesting sites on product ideas:

http://www.kadaza.com/

Click on any of the categories and you will find x amount of websites in that niche. For example if you look under the Tech category (http://www.kadaza.com/tech) you will find "**The Gadget Flow**". By subscribing to their newsletter you get weekly updates on trendy items (that may not even be on Amazon yet). Lets take a look at an example:

Just a few days ago I received an email from The Gadget Flow. Its a site that I subscribe to among many others. I found the site by looking trough above Kadaza links.

So when I opened the email there were a lot of products that are currently on sites like Kickstarter or other similar sites. But you know what? If its only on Kickstarter now it means it isn't on Amazon yet hence you can take the product idea and even improve on it. So I looked at the first product that caught my attention (lots of other good ideas too in that email):

After clicking on the link I found that the company is based in Denmark and funded their product "the Sitpack" successfully on Kickstarter.

Just a quick search on Alibaba.com and I immediately find a supplier:

As you can see the supplier either stole the pictures or he is the actual producer for this company. I think it is the first one but it could be that they are the sole manufacturer.

Now I go on Amazon and see that there is only one seller, the actual company "Sitpack" selling for 149$!!! Look at the listing. So much to improve!!

Also I am pretty sure that this product does not cost more than 10$ to manufacture. Wow what a margin!

Either way, the point I want to get to you is not to copy these companies but find ideas on blog sites (subscribe to them) and see how quick and easy you can research suppliers on Alibaba or Globalsources for suppliers. Maybe add an accessory, change colors or whatever you feel could improve the product. The best thing about subscribing to these sites is that you get ideas delivered for free to your email address.

3) Exhibitions

One of my favorite and most efficient way to find new products is at exhibitions. There are hundreds of exhibitions each year in many countries. You get to meet the supplier, see the products, and talk over details such as prices, models, and much more. On top of all of that I guarantee you that you will get inspired. To find exhibitions near you just Google the exhibition center near you and get your entry ticket. Most times you will need to provide name cards and contact details for that. You can order business cards for $5 these days. Going to an exhibition prepared and with a professional image gives the supplier a great impression of you.

There are countless exhibitions around Asia throughout the year but mostly during April and October. Here is a list of exhibitions for October 2016:

http://www.globalsources.com/NEWS/TRADE_SHOW_CALENDA R_OCTOBER2016_A.pdf

A great write up from one of webretailers earlier posts of Danny McMillan who I had the pleasure of meeting in Hong Kong in April: http://www.webretailer.com/lean-commerce/sourcing-trip-china/

4) Supermarkets, shopping malls

Another way to find new products is obviously when you are out in a shopping mall or a local shop. To start your own import business means that you also work when you are out with friends/family at a shopping mall. Keep your eyes open and when you see something cool make a reminder for yourself on your smart phone to look the product up later.

5) Tools

A) Junglescout

You have probably heard of Junglescout already. Junglescout is probably the most advanced tool when it comes to navigating Amazon and finding bestseller products. Jungle Scout integrates into your Google Chrome browser, streamlining your product research. Extract rank, sales volume, FBA fee's, type and quantity and a lot more!

I had the chance to meeet Junglescout's founder Greg Mercer twice. He is a really cool and down to earth guy who seems to work purely for the community. Check out his blog and site where you can get hundreds of product ideas itself if not using his tool.

B) Cashcowpro

In 2016 this year I was contacted by Antoni Watts, the founder of CashCowPro. I looked up his tool and was amazed by how he has probably put together the most comprehensive tool that not only helps to boost sales but also provides accurate insightful metrics for selling on Amazon. From all the tools out there I think this is my favorite when it comes to keeping track of all my sales as well as testing features.

It also works also iPhone and Android APP. Within the tool there is a Top 100,000 NICHE selector... They actually scanned over 100 million products + ASINs on Amazon to create this list.

They automatically calculate the factory cost and Air + Sea freight to give you the Top 100,000 most profitable NICHES on Amazon. Not products, but actual NICHES, using the average of the TOP 5 ranking products for each Niche to calculate the overall performance. The tool has many more functions apart from the niche selector that you can see here:

https://www.youtube.com/watch?v=rATKSmj1bcg

6) Travelling

Travelling is also a great way to find ideas. When you are out of your country or state you will likely see items that your country/state does not have. There could be many reasons why they may not be available where you live, but it's always worth it to check an idea out. I remember when my friend told me about 10 years ago about Bubble Tea & Fancy Green Tea drinks sold in Hong Kong and Asia. She was from Germany and she had never seen these drinks back home. She didn't go on any further with that idea but a few years later back in Germany these drinks started to pop up and were a smashing hit! So even when you think at first that idea might be nothing, it could be worth millions! Share the idea with a few friends and brainstorm about it.

7) Alibaba & Globalsources

A) Alibaba

First off when you sign up on Alibaba you generally need to fill in which product categories you are interested in. Based on this criteria and your recent product searches on Alibaba you'll get automated emails with new product deals. Als you can subscribe look in their "selection site" where they post a lot of the newest and trendiest items from their suppliers:

http://selection.alibaba.com/?spm=a2700.7848340.0.0.tevCsV&tracelog=hd_cor_selection

B) Globalsources

Pretty much the same with Globalsources. You sign up and get automated emails with great product deals here. But not enough, they also have a section with the best deals and newest products out of every product category: Top Products. And my favourite part are their eMagazines that are updated on a monthly basis with the hottest and newest product alerts on their site.

Check out the links listed above and browse trough hundreds of products. Use the techniques and step by step scenario as described above depending on your situation.

Some more ideas on how to find the "perfect" product also in one of my earlier guest blog posts from Thomas Albiez based in Switzerland: https://importdojo.com/how-to-find-the-perfect-product-2/

Once thing I can recommend everyone at some point is to come to Asia and visit some of the exhibitions. I feel it is just the most efficient way to find products.

I know it may not be cheap to come here but I can guarantee its worth it. A plane ticket and a few nights at a cheap hotel can go from $1500. But you'll see actual suppliers, products and samples in real. Saving you a lot of money and time in the process. Here are a few impressions fand trip reports from my times at the exhibitions:

https://importdojo.com/news-and-trends-from-the-exhibitions-in-asia/
https://importdojo.com/news-and-trends-from-the-exhibition-april-2016/

CHAPTER 7
VALIDATE YOUR PRODUCT IDEA

You've found your product, GREAT! But careful, don't get over excited about a product that you just found or had an idea for. You need to evaluate first if your product fits the market and its consumers.

We call this **"product-to-market-fit,"** meaning you have something that the market really needs.

To evaluate your product you should go through the following steps:

COSTS:

- Cost of manufacturing
- Cost of transport. This can be crucial to your margin if the transport cost is very high.
- Cost of duties and taxes
- Possible profit before tax

COMPETITION:
- Make sure no one or not many people carry your product.
- Analyze the market, do your research. Look at social media hash tags:
- Test the idea with a few forums (but don't give away too much information)
- Research trends on blog sites (such as Shopify.com)

More great tips available on Shopify:

http://www.shopify.com/blog/12932121-what-to-sell-online-8-strategies-for-finding-your-first-product

CHAPTER 8
WAYS TO PRODUCT SOURCING

I think there are generally three effective ways to source your product:

- **Internet** (Alibaba, Globalsources, Aliexpress, HKTDC)
- **Exhibitions / Conventions**
- **Contacts**

Internet:

The Internet is probably the fastest way to source for products.

There are hundreds of providers on the Internet to source for products.

The most reliable and efficient ones would be:

ALIBABA (B2B-Business to Business for larger quantities)

ALIEXPRESS (B2C Business to Consumer for small order and drop shipment)

GLOBALSOURCES (B2B and Marketplace) Alibaba's competitor in Hong Kong

HKTDC.COM (B2B with small order and drop shipment) from Hong Kong

I mainly use Alibaba or Globalsources since they have been around the longest and are the safest to use.

There are many other websites within China similar to those two but they are not as user friendly and safe. For some of them, including

TAOBAO or BAIDU, you would need to speak Chinese or hire a translator.

Exhibitions/Conventions

I would say exhibitions are the most effective way to find suppliers and products since you meet face to face and can also see the products.

As a first step Internet sourcing is fine, but maybe try to arrange your next China trip around an exhibition.

I learned, after many disappointments, that you don't want to place a large order (more than 100 pieces) without knowing what you will get. You wouldn't want to place an order with someone you never met and transfer a lot of money to him. So going to exhibitions helps a lot.

Tip:
Even if you can't go to an exhibition you can still find out about all the suppliers exhibiting there. How? Simply go onto the exhibition's website. For example, this lighting fair in Hong Kong: http://www.hktdc.com/fair/hklightingfairae-en/HKTDC-Hong-Kong-International-Lighting-Fair-Autumn-Edition.html.

Then click on **"Full Exhibitor List"** and there you go. You have all exhibitors exhibiting at this fair. It's a bit of a lengthy process but you can check all websites of the suppliers, look at their products, and contact them directly without even going to the exhibition.

As I mentioned already, in this section we focus on the exhibitions in Asia. I would say there are three major organizers and hosts that cover EVERYTHING that you need. You need to preregister with all three organizers and it's FREE of CHARGE.

Main Exhibition Organizers in China/Hong Kong:

HKTDC

www.hktdc.com

HKTDC covers most of the fairs held in Hong Kong. All exhibitions are held at the Wan Chai convention center on Hong Kong Island. Hong Kong exhibitions will also be the most important ones for you (apart from Canton Fair). They cover everything from jewelry to food to electronics, gifts, optical, maritime, and much more. Click on the link and see all the upcoming events. HKTDC's events usually have the big names exhibiting. That's a good way to spot trends and innovative products. But eventually you want to buy from the factories with lower prices.

GLOBALSOURCES

www.globalsources.com

Globalsources is the second organizer in Hong Kong. They exhibit at the Asia World Expo Hall at the Hong Kong International Airport. They also cover the most product categories (electronics, jewelry, textiles, and more). The events are usually smaller in size and the exhibiting suppliers are mostly cheaper than at HKTDC. Having said that I personally feel that Globalsources organizes the best shows within HK due to their professionalism.

CANTON FAIR

http://www.cantonfair.org.cn/en/

The Canton Fair is the holy grail of exhibitions. This event is so large that it is held twice a year and each time runs over a span of 3½ weeks in three different phases. Each phase comes with different product categories. As of 2016 there were over 26,000 exhibitors. This exhibition is a must for me and it should be for you too. You will find a lot of innovations, big brands, small factories, or the product you have been looking for for so long.

Plan at least 2, or better 3, days for your product category/phase. Sign up once and get a badge that will be valid forever.

> **Tip:** Don't throw away your badge. You can use it for your next visit without paying 100 Yuan for a replacement card.

CONTACTS:

Last but not least, contacts that you already have can be very helpful. Ask around in your friend circle, relatives, and so on. You never know, your sister's cousin might have a contact that you didn't know about.

Sign up on business networks such as www.linkedin.com if you haven't already. You can find a lot on there and can ask around if anyone has any contacts to suppliers for your products.

There are also professional groups on those two websites with lots of suppliers offering their services. Simply search for a group that could meet your needs (e.g., consumer electronics suppliers / textile suppliers, etc.) and post your inquiry to this specific group.

If you aren't on any business networks or have no contacts, I recommend that you start with Alibaba/Aliexpress.

Usually, government agencies in your country will also provide you with supplier contacts. But be aware, most of these contacts will likely be importers themselves. You will want to cut them out and go to the source. Remember, that's what this course is all about.

CHAPTER 9
ALIBABA AND GLOBALSOURCES

We have covered important groundwork and the necessary steps to successful importing.

Now let's get to one of the most important parts of finding products and suppliers.

ALIBABA AND GLOBALSOURCES

ALIBABA:

If you don't have contacts the easiest way is to start looking at www.alibaba.com.

Alibaba is also relatively simple to use.

You create an account, fill in your company information and details, and then you can start sourcing right away.

You can filter by products or suppliers. Nowadays it's pretty safe to use Alibaba. Most suppliers are pre-assessed by Alibaba through document checking, phone calls, and various other methods. Some suppliers even have on-site checks, which means that a third-party did a factory audit and you can actually download that audit.

There are many other cool functions, such as filtering by country or region. Say you plan on going to Shenzhen or Guangzhou. You can narrow down the province in filters (in this case Guangdong province), so you only see suppliers from that region.

Most products are made in specific areas.

Here are a few examples:

- **Guangdong province** (South of China): Electronics of any kind, especially consumer and household, toys
- **Zhejiang province** (Shanghai area): DIY products, tools, metals and fabrics, lighting
- **Hebei province** (Beijing area): Textiles, coal, steel, iron, engineering, chemicals, power, ceramics, and food.

Section 1) Begin your search:

This is fairly straightforward. You can browse two options, products and suppliers.

We will start with products since we are assuming we don't know the supplier.

We are looking at a Bluetooth speaker.

Wow, over 1,000,000 products!!

Bear in mind, many of them are duplicates because of multiple entries by the same supplier. Also, you will often find that popular and openly available products are offered by different suppliers.

Insider tip: It's also very easy to tell the trading companies, middle men, and scammers from the real factories.

How? Simple. In the middle of the columns I can filter by:

Gold supplier: This is a paid membership from Alibaba for the supplier. They get featured and can put up a lot more items in their catalogue (among other functions).

Onsite Check: The onsite operation of the factory has been checked by Alibaba and a third party confirmed its legal existence.

Assessed supplier: This is a third-party assessment usually done through a testing company to verify various parts of the company. This includes machinery, staff, engineers, workers, certification, and much more.

So how do I tell if it's a trading company, an illegitimate company, or a real factory? Simple. Trading or fake companies would not be a

Gold Supplier or have an onsite check done, and they would not be assessed by a third party. **First,** it's quite an investment for the supplier promoting his service (Alibaba doesn't pay anything), and **second,** if this third party arrives at the address to check the factory they won't find anything but three guys sitting in a small office selling items from the real factory at higher prices.

Alibaba unfortunately has hundreds of middlemen and scammers that pose as manufacturers. Many of these "manufacturers" are not manufacturers at all, rather middlemen that pose as such, marking up the price and increasing the level of miscommunication between you and the actual manufacturer while providing little, if any real value.

With these filters you can pretty much eliminate middlemen, trading companies, scammers, and so on. Unfortunately, you will also eliminate real factories that are either new to Alibaba or do not make the effort of going through all stages of verification. If your search did not conclude anything in the first step, then you can perhaps extend the list again by unchecking "on-site check" or "assessed supplier" and looking through your options with Gold Suppliers first.

Moving on, through filtering I now "only" have 165,000 products to choose from. I naturally look at the first one and a few others that interest me in terms of design/color, etc.

This supplier uses nice photos, provides crucial details and specifications, and even test reports at the end.

The second supplier also uses nice photos, a clear description, and a clean look.

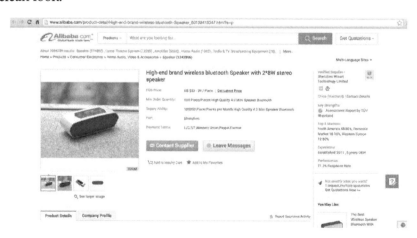

So what do I look for now and how do I go on?

A) The price

One of the first things you'll look at is the price. For this listing we can see a price of $30-60 USD FOB. FOB stands for Free On Board and means that the seller will pay all involved costs that get the product to the nearest port. This would be the most viable way to ship goods from Asia. The buyer pays the cost of actually transporting the goods across the ocean to the final destination. The price here is not really relevant as it is most likely just a place holder.

B) Minimum Order Quantity (MOQ)

We look at the minimum order quantity. The minimum order quantity (MOQ) is the smallest order the manufacturer is willing to accept to start production. However, it's important to note that this is almost always negotiable. In our example, the minimum order is nine units. I highly doubt that this is the MOQ. In this case it usually means that they have stock and you can buy from nine pieces. But for mass production (and cheaper prices) they probably have a MOQ of 100 pieces or more.

C) Payment Options

There are several common methods of payment, and each have their pros and cons for both the buyer and the seller. The longer you work with a supplier the easier it will be to deal with payments. If you have an established business relationship you could ask that the next order should be paid 100% on delivery (TT). He can always say no, but if he agrees this gives you financial liquidity.

Let's take a look at the most common payment options and the associated risk level to you as the buyer:

1. TT (Telegraphic Bank Transfer)

Risk Level For Buyer: Medium Risk

With a bank transfer, the supplier will receive payment before production starts. Very important: if you agree to this payment, **NEVER** pay more than 30% upfront. Seventy percent will be paid upon inspection and shipment release. This payment method bears a high level of risk to the buyer and generally is not recommended when dealing with an unknown supplier. There is little that can be done to get your money back if something goes wrong.

2. Letter of Credit (L/C)

Risk Level For Buyer: Very Safe

A letter of credit is safe for both parties. However a letter of credit is rather complicated to issue through a bank, costs quite a lot of money, and is generally only recommended for larger purchases ($20,000 and above).

3. Western Union

Risk Level For Buyer: Very Risky

Western Union generally should only be used when dealing with people you know very well. There is no guarantee if something goes wrong.

4. PayPal

Risk Level For Buyer: Fairly Safe

PayPal is a popular payment method for buyers as it presents a much lower risk, ease of use, and generally pretty good buyer protection. Although it's a popular option with buyers, it's less popular with suppliers due to difficulties in withdrawing money, high tax rates, and potential charge backs from less than honest buyers.

5. Escrow

Risk Level For Buyer: Very Safe

When using an escrow service, the buyer's money is held by a third party and is only paid to the supplier after the buyer confirms satisfactory delivery of their order. Escrow is a fairly safe payment method for buying and selling online because it protects both the buyer and supplier.

You can read about common payment methods on Alibaba on the Alibaba Safe Buying page.

http://www.alibaba.com/help/safety_security/class/buying/pay_ship/0 02.html

Generally, when you are just starting, you'll probably want to look for or negotiate with suppliers to either accept PayPal or some type of escrow service to give you the highest level of protection.

The next step would be to start communicating with the supplier.

D) Contacting Suppliers

Introduce yourself to each supplier professionally. When I first contact a supplier it usually looks like this. You can copy this section and use it for your first contact:

Dear...,

My name is ..... and I am the ....(Manager/President/Buyer etc.) of .... Limited/Inc.

We are a (fill in your company's business, e.g., Importer/Buying Office/Whole seller/Online shop) and are operating in (fill in your country).

You can also check out our website under: www. ......

I am writing to you today to inquire about the product I saw on your website/catalogue/exhibition.

The model number is....

Could you please give me the following information: You can fill in the details in the attached quotation format or send me your quotation in the first step.

Unit price based on.... Pieces
Minimum Order Quantity
Available certification (CE, RoHS, FCC, GS, etc.)
Production lead-time
Available colors
Payment terms

I would then evaluate and get back to you as soon as possible. If you have any questions please don't hesitate to contact me.

Thanks and best regards,

E) TIPS WHEN CONTACTING SUPPLIERS:

Do this step with **multiple suppliers**, because it's never good when you start to rely on just one supplier.

Do not mention that this is your first time contacting suppliers on Alibaba. It will probably give you a disadvantage in negotiating at a later point.

For easier reference and **keeping track of your offers and suppliers** I recommend making yourself a folder on your desktop. Name it

"Alibaba" or "Sourcing" or anything that you can relate to easily. Create subfolders for each supplier. In each subfolder create folders such as: "quotation," "supplier profile," "certificates," and so on.

Within this course we will provide simple offer sheets and supplier profile forms that you can include in your email when sending to the supplier for the first time.

Also, I have found that some suppliers don't read your full email. So **point out the model number** that you are interested in and ask them to quote specifically.

Sometimes you will receive a simple email back with a PDF catalogue asking which item you are interested in. It can be exasperating but that's the way it is sometimes. Politely reply back that you are **"looking for a specific quote on model number…"**

You don't necessarily have to use these forms for contacting the supplier for the first time. Many will actually not fill it in because it obviously takes time to do so.

HOWEVER, I recommend if you have narrowed down your suppliers you should ask them to fill it in for your records. Keeping clean records is crucial to your follow-up.

F) Ask questions and follow up

As you begin narrowing down suppliers make sure to ask a lot of questions about their business and their products:

Ask for a copy of their business license and company and factory standards (for example ISO-9001)

Ask which laboratories/third party companies they work with. If they only work with Chinese test or inspection companies be cautious.

Ask for photos of the factory or company presentation (PDF/PowerPoint) and sample products.

Feel free to ask for whatever makes you feel more comfortable doing business with them. Ask who their customers are and where they are located. If they don't have any customers in your country be careful, as they might have no experience dealing with your country's regulations and standards. Ask about them. If they already work with a competitor of yours or with an industry similar to yours it's a good sign that they can fulfill your requirements.

Send a vendor profile so they can fill in their details. They should cover production capability, how many workers/staff/engineers, main customers, certifications, company turnover, etc.

G) Get samples

It should go without saying that before you invest any significant amount of money into inventory you need to get samples to check and verify quality. We explain the sample process in Chapter 10.

H). Sounds fishy!

Finally, if something is too good to be true, it usually is. Be aware of prices, suspicious payments, or communication that doesn't seem right. It's never too late to simply cease communication and look for another supplier.

> **Tip:** When asking your questions and formatting your emails to suppliers it's best to work with paragraphs or bullet lists of requests so that it is easy for them to understand your requirements and needs. Make the supplier answer each of your "bullet-questions."

I) Requesting a quotation

Requesting a quotation/price, also referred to as a RFQ (request for quote) is a relatively simple process. However, taking a few extra minutes to plan your email can make a significant difference in the number and quality of replies you receive.

Here again is a simple form for a RFQ:

Dear...,

My name is ..... and I am the ....(Manager/President/Buyer etc.) of .... Limited/Inc.

We are a (fill in your company's business, e.g., Importer/Buying Office/Whole seller/Online shop) and are operating in (fill in your country).

You can also check out our website under: www. .....

I am writing to you today to inquire about the product I saw on your website/catalogue/exhibition.

The model number is....

Could you please give me the following information: You can fill in the details in the attached quotation format or send me your quotation in the first step.

Unit price based on .... Pieces
Minimum Order Quantity
Available certification (CE, RoHS, FCC, GS, etc.)
Production lead time
Available colors
Payment terms

I would then evaluate and get back to you as soon as possible.
If you have any questions please don't hesitate to contact me.

Thanks and best regards

J) Negotiating

Once you have begun conversations with multiple suppliers and have a good idea about their prices, MOQ's, and payment terms, you can begin negotiating with them.

Here are some tips on negotiating:

It is a given that once you place your order you negotiate the price, whether you are below the supplier's MOQ or not.

Use the price that you were originally quoted and decrease it by 20%. Give this target price to the factory and let them know you would like to order with your (20% reduced) price. In most cases, the supplier will not agree to your new target price but he may reduce it by another 5%.

In 80% of cases he will give you a further reduction on his original quoted price, unless your quantity is really very low.

Also, mention to him that this will be the first trial order and that if it is successful larger orders will follow.

K) Weighing Your Options

Once you've narrowed it down to a select few suppliers, you'll want to weigh all your options. Bear in mind it's not always about the price and MOQ. It's also a gut feeling that you should get when communicating with a supplier. Did he reply eagerly and quickly? Did he follow up in detail or just send fragments to your questions? If you have the feeling it's difficult now to communicate, imagine how it would be to work with him once the order is placed. Make sure you eliminate the suppliers with the least potential and the most issues now!

Conclusion for ALIBABA

Sourcing a reliable supplier for your product from Alibaba can be a great experience. Following the above steps and tips should get you working with a reliable and good supplier. Don't just settle on your first supplier or only one supplier. Keep your options open and order multiple quotations and perhaps samples.

GLOBALSOURCES

Global Sources is very similar to Alibaba. It's just a bit smaller and less known.

Sometimes when I don't find a product on Alibaba I go to Global Sources, or vice versa. What I like about Global Sources is that their customer follow up is usually better than Alibaba's. I guess that's because they are located in Hong Kong, while Alibaba is based in Hangzhou (China), so their customer support is usually in a better English.

Start by registering and creating a profile as a buyer. It's the same process you followed with Alibaba.

Once you have completed your registration you can start looking for products and suppliers.

Once you have input your product search you will see suppliers and products.

On the right they have a nice tool that is similar to those in Alibaba. You can see if the supplier has been verified, which customers he has, does he exhibit, and so on.

You can also filter by "manufacturer," "locations," and much more. Again, it's very similar to Alibaba.

Check out all their features such as Magazines, Tradeshows, Marketplace and more. There is a LOT of free information on there. I personally really love their e-magazines. There are a lot of suppliers in there with great photos, contact information, and much more. This is only available as a registered user though.

Start your product search as under Section 1 on Alibaba in the previous chapter.

CHAPTER 10
ORDERING SAMPLES

It goes without saying that you shouldn't place a large order without ever having seen a sample or product. You need to test your sample for function, durability, and more.

When ordering samples most suppliers will charge you. And the majority of those will charge 20-50% on top of the regular price, because making a sample is more "costly." The actual reason they charge more is because they are afraid you only want to order a sample and then never come back.

Either way, this is an investment you need to make.

> **Insider Tip:** Most suppliers will refund you the cost of the sample on the first order. So make sure to remind the supplier of this when you place an actual order.

Tips on sending/receiving samples:

1) When you ask for a sample, you don't want it to be caught up in customs. There are a few items that may not be sent via airmail or courier, such as items with a built-in battery (e.g., power banks to charge mobile phones). Check with your carrier or local post office on that.

2) Ask the supplier to state: "samples of no commercial value" on the sample invoice that is packed with the sample. This way, customs will see this is a sample not to be resold and should therefore not be taxed.

3) Ask the supplier to lower the value of the sample cost on the invoice. BUT it shouldn't be an amount that is too low; if it is it may sound not credible. For example, if you order an item that is sold to you at 9USD, then the declared amount should not be lower than 3USD. If you have an item that is obviously expensive then make sure you don't set the amount too low (e.g., real value 99USD, but declared value 8USD).

4) In some cases large sample orders will be held at customs, mainly because samples with a value that is declared too low arises suspicion. You may have to pay the tax and duties.

When you order a sample with the factory make sure of the following steps:

- **Send an email inquiry on how many pieces you would like**
- **State the color and describe what the sample should look like (based on the supplier's offer)**
- **State the address it should be sent to**
- **Make sure the supplier states "samples of no-commercial value"**
- **Tell the supplier that you will deduct the sample charge from your first order**
- **Declare a proper amount of sample value**

CHAPTER 11
TESTING YOUR SAMPLES

Once you receive your samples it is time to perform a visual inspection and a functioning test. Whether your sample is of a textile nature, an electric product, or a decorative item, make sure you test it. Bend it, stretch it, use it, and test how it functions. Often I receive samples and they are so difficult to figure out (for example electronics) as they are not user friendly at all.

How can your customers understand and use your product in a simple way when you can't? Make sure that your item is easy to handle for everyone and that it comes with an instruction manual (if applicable).

You don't need to be an engineer to test simple functions. If you do have a friend or colleague who knows technical things hand the sample to him and let him give you an honest opinion.

If you found anything that you would like to change or have explained ask your supplier to look into this, either to improve the product quality or give you feedback on any problem. Make sure that the supplier will improve any problems and indicate to him that (in case of an order) you will test this during the inspection (performed by third party, Chapter 21).

CHAPTER 12
GENERAL PRODUCT REQUIREMENTS

This goes with the previous chapter.

Larger retailers or buying companies usually have their sample tested professionally before placing an order. This is done either by their internal lab or a third party. If you would like to make absolutely sure that your product conforms to regulations and is up to quality standards take this step. It will usually cost you a few hundred USD, depending on the third party. I recommend this step if your item is costly and your quantity is larger than 500 pieces or 2000USD in total value. You will usually receive a test report that you could also send to your supplier and ask for his feedback or improvement of the product before order placement.

Today there are many basic requirements that need to be met. For example, chemical substances in plastic or textiles are not allowed to exceed a certain amount within the product. Some items need to have a certain certificate (such as FCC, RoHS or CE), which means that the product is preapproved under certain criteria and OK to import.

Of all the smaller companies that drop-ship or have smaller order quantities I know for a fact that 95% of them don't have their items tested for chemical substances or other technical requirements. If you drop-ship directly to your customers (for example FBA-fulfillment by Amazon) you won't get into trouble. But if you are selling to larger companies or wholesalers they will probably ask you for test reports.

If you (or the third party) found anything that you would like to change or have explained ask your supplier to look into this, either to improve the product quality or give you feedback on any problem. Make sure that the supplier will fix any problems, and indicate to him that (in case of an order) you will test again during the inspection (performed by third party, Chapter 23).

Bear in mind if you are a start-up or planning your first import this step may not be necessary as it adds cost to your product.

However, if you have an existing business and are trying to expand into larger importing this is an absolute must.

Depending on your product you can check general requirements here:

http://importdojo.com/import-dojo-certification/

Under above link you will find my latest release on my certification course.

What is it all about?

Amazon and other sales channels are getting a lot of pressure from authorities to make their sellers comply to laws.

So far Amazon has only stated on their training pages that sellers must comply with regulations and standards when selling on Amazon. Have a look here:

It is the seller's responsibility to comply with all U.S. customs laws and regulations, including applicable duty and tax requirements. Import duty and taxes are due when importing goods into the United States whether by a private individual or a commercial entity. Some goods are not subject to duty. U.S. Customs and Border Protection does not require an importer to have a license or permit. Other agencies may require a permit, license, or other certification, depending on what is being imported.

Note: It is your responsibility to ensure all goods comply with applicable regulatory requirements.

Now that you have an idea of where you'd like to expand your business, it's time to explore how taxes and regulations might affect your business for each marketplace in which you intend to sell. This section provides an overview by region of the taxes and regulations you should be aware of when selling in Amazon's various marketplaces and enlisting third-party resources. We recommend that you consult your tax and regulatory advisors before making decisions about how you will sell in other marketplaces.

Every country has legal and industry requirements concerning sales of products to consumers. In your home marketplace, there are probably laws that pertain to intellectual property rights, product safety, environmental, and other applicable requirements. The same is true for all marketplaces. Do your research and understand your responsibilities. Some things to consider are:

- Tax and customs
- Intellectual property rights
- Parallel importation
- Export controls
- Markings and labels
- Environmental, Health, and Safety
- Product compliance

Taxes and regulations with Amazon Global Selling

- United States Tax and Regulatory Considerations
- Canada tax and regulatory considerations
- Europe Tax and Regulatory Considerations
- Japan Tax and Regulatory Considerations
- Mexico Tax and Regulatory Considerations
- New Zealand Goods and Services Tax (GST)
- Russian VAT Frequently Asked Questions
- International Trade Laws

Category requirements

- Sellers must have an active Professional selling plan. Learn more about Seller account features.
- Sellers must conduct proper research to ensure that their Industrial & Scientific product listings comply with applicable local, state, federal, and international laws and regulations.
- All products must meet North America product safety standards. For more information, visit the U.S. Consumer Product Safety Commission and Health Canada's Consumer Product Safety resources.
- Sellers should only list Industrial & Scientific Supplies in the Industrial & Scientific Category. Listing of products that are not Industrial or Scientific supplies will result in removal of seller approval to list in this category.

Product considerations

When you select an Amazon marketplace in which to sell, you'll need to understand whether your product is appropriate for your target country. First and foremost, make sure that you comply with all laws in each country. In addition, product standards differ across countries. For example, MP3 players operating on 110-220 V that use two-prong electrical chargers may not be appropriate for the UK marketplace but could be appropriate for Japan. Similarly, feather beds you successfully sell in the UK would probably not sell well in the United States because the standard mattress sizes are different in each country.

For more details, review product restrictions and other requirements in Taxes and Regulations.

PAY ATTENTION
to standards and requirements

Did you ever read this part or just flew over it quickly….

Did you ever import a product and it got stuck at customs because it did not have the right certificates or labeling requirement that are needed for imports in your country?

I hope not, because this can really cost you thousands of dollars. Amazon and other sales channels will ban sellers that do not comply with standards. Your eCommerce journey will be over before you know it.

Let's face it. Dealing with certifications and test reports isn't the most fun thing to do but over the last 7 months I've worked on a course that will help you to navigate the jungle of rules and regulations, give you actionable advice what you need and show you how to use certificates to get a clear competitive edge in todays overcrowded markets. I also give you examples where you don't need to test, how you can save money and when to walk away from a certain product or supplier.

This alone will help you to save thousands of dollars and by getting the right certifications and tests you can ensure compliance with all mandatory safety standards & labelling requirements for Europe and North America.

With the growing health consciousness of customers the right certification and compliance can give you a clear and competitive edge.

Have you ever worried about test reports, customs and what national laws and standards you need to meet when you buy a product from China?

Then this is the course for you. In this course I walk you through all the standards and laws there are out there for the US and the European Union.

I explain all the basics to give you a better understanding what you need to meet legally, where you can save money and how to find the right standard for your product.

I explain in laymen's terms what all these standards mean and how you can simply comply to them.

The best part is I've done all the work for you. I provide you with actionable PDF's for 27 product categories that give you a clear picture of all the regulations that a certain product falls into.

Be it electronics, kitchen, garden, toys or furniture's. I explain each PDF or Product Requirement Profile and all you have to do when you source from China is to send this PDF to your chosen suppliers and ask them if they can fulfill your requirements.

I give examples in each PDF that apply to all product categories.

For example if you are not sure what your kitchen helper has to meet in terms of standards and compliance you just have to look at the PDF that I prepared for you, look at the country requirements, laws and certifications and ask your supplier if he can meet them.

You don't have to look any further and dig trough the internet and read hundreds of authority or government websites still not knowing what standard you have to meet.

I also give you case studies on different product groups and how I find out what certification they need to meet. You'll get contacts of test laboratories and how you can contact them and get your product tested.

Have you ever worried that a suppliers gives you a fake certificate? Look no further, I explain how you can find out if a supplier is sending you fake certificates or not. This will help you filter out the good from the bad ones.

With this course you'll get a practical roadmap to ensure compliance with all mandatory safety standards & labelling requirements for Europe and North America.

There is a step by step process to do all this and this is what you are going to learn here. Again, have a look here and find out more:

https://importdojo.com/import-dojo-certification/

Finding inspection and third party companies that can tell you what needs to be fulfilled is covered in Chapter 23.

CHAPTER 13
OEM /ODM PRODUCTS

You will also need to know what different types of products there are. There are open **(ODM)** and closed products **(OEM)**. **OEM** stands for **"original equipment manufacturer"** and ODM stands for **"original design manufacturer."**

This is vital knowledge for your product sourcing. You need to know the difference between these two. Anything that can be found on Alibaba or Gloabalsources is usually **ODM.**

OEM:

When you see a big brand product, for example Apple's iPhone or Samsung's S6, that is OEM. It means that Apple/Samsung designed something and has an exclusive contract with the manufacturer that does not allow the manufacturer to sell the product to anyone else. It's an Apple/Samsung-owned design and theirs only.

That also means that Apple probably paid the supplier all the costs to make the tooling for the products. Usually toolings are very expensive. Small parts like a cover or a case can cost easily 2000USD. Toolings are necessary for production are manufacturing. A raw material will be crafted through the tooling and will eventually become the product's part.

OEM products are usually not showcased on a manufacturer's website/exhibition or even showroom. The manufacturer is not allowed to show it to the customer.

The advantage of OEM is that you alone own the design, and no one else can. The disadvantage is that there is a lot of pre-investment involved. I recommend this option only if you have the available funds/backup from your customer (for example crowd-sourcing website Kickstarter.com) or you are willing to invest yourself because you strongly believe in your design.

OEM should also cover a **non-disclosure-agreement (NDA)** with your supplier prohibiting him or any of his employees to discuss your designs, prototypes, or product developments. We will cover that in the second part of this book in more detail. In the first step you may not want to do OEM as you are just starting out.

Keep in mind that:

- Not every supplier is open to OEM
- Investment is large
- Long delivery times (tooling can take up to 60 days and manufacturing another 40-60 days)
- Large quantities are involved
- Your product is unique and owned by you

ODM:

This means that the tooling is probably designed and owned by the factory (or they paid someone to do it). They can sell their product and design to whomever they want to. That means when you go to an exhibition anyone can buy the showcased product.

This option has its advantages and disadvantages. The advantage is you don't need to invest in any tooling and you can buy an item off the rack from the supplier. You can change colors or use your own branding but that's the extent of what you can change.

The disadvantage is obviously that everyone else can buy it too, you don't have a unique product.

This option is the most used option to source and buy products in China. It's easy, there is no design or investment involved (apart from order costs), small quantities can be bought from the manufacturer, and the delivery can be fast.

Keep in mind that:

- Small order quantities
- Everyone can buy it
- Shorter delivery times

Some suppliers are willing to do the investment for OEM for you. But that's usually only if you have worked with them before and done more than 100,000USD worth of business with them.

Here is an option on how to get your design made (OEM) without investment:

Insider tip: If you do not have the capital to invest in OEM but your supplier has, discuss with him that he invests first, you can have exclusivity for a year, and then he is allowed to sell it to everyone. Do this **ONLY** if you absolutely believe in your product. The supplier will want to have a sales guarantee from you in a separate exclusivity contract.

CHAPTER 14
PAYMENT AND DELIVERY

Incoterms:

The Incoterms rules or **International Commercial Terms are the way you pay and have your goods delivered. Please look at this very detailed entry on Wikipedia**:

http://en.wikipedia.org/wiki/Incoterms

When any supplier from China gives you an offer it's usually **FOB** (Free On Board).

FOB means that he produces and ships the items once manufactured to the nearest port. His responsibility ends there and you (or your logistics provider) take care of the rest. This is the most used option when importing from Asia. There are many different other options that may suit you more, depending on your budget and experience in shipping. See the Incoterms above for more options. Discuss with your supplier or forwarder how you would like your goods to be shipped.

The longer you work with a supplier the easier it will be to deal with payments. If you have an established business relationship you can ask that the next order should be paid 100% on delivery (TT). He can always say no, but if he agrees this gives you financial liquidity.

CHAPTER 15
HOW TO BUILD A RELATIONSHIP WITH MANUFACTURERS

Your suppliers are critical to your business success. The better you treat them the more they are willing to continue business with you and give you better service or performance than their other customers.

I have found that suppliers give better treatment and pay more attention to a customer's order (crucial for you) when they **get treated fairly**.

You think the supplier was just waiting for your business? Think again.

Established suppliers usually have a long queue of customers waiting for them.

They are more likely to give priority to customers where they make more margin and to ones that are easier to deal with.

In my previous job I had buyers who were very aggressive and tried to squeeze every cent out of the supplier. It was very difficult to handle these buyers and often I couldn't find a suitable supplier for them. Even after orders were fulfilled these buyers would often come afterwards and try to claim money for a "faulty" product when there was actually nothing wrong. Many times just for the sake of it they would try to get money out of the supplier. This is not the way I work with my factories.

I believe in a fair **respectful and trusting** relationship with suppliers.

You'll get what you put in. Want cheap? Get cheap. I guess it all depends on what type of product you are looking for. If you are in for fighting with competitors on Amazon or EbayEbay you are probably looking for the cheapest there is. But don't be surprised when your products are of poor quality and you get bombed with bad reviews on Amazon/EbayEbay. If you want to stand out from your competition you might as well start with good quality products perhaps at a higher price. Sure, once in a while you look for the absolute price entry product, but be prepared on the quality issues.

Also, I gain nothing from **squeezing my supplier** out of every cent when he is struggling to fulfill the order and pay his workers. What if I want to place a reorder or need a favor one day? He may not be around anymore and I'll be stuck.

In times when a supplier is in trouble because of another customer you may want to help him. Say he has produced a lot of product that another customer cancelled. I may even refer some customers to him. Trust me, this kind of relationship is very valuable for you. If you help him he may offer free samples, discounts on your next order, and so on.

I would say there are six rules to having a great relationship with your supplier:

1. **Make sure there are mutual benefits**
2. **Respect each other**
3. **Be fair to each other**
4. **Trust one another**
5. **Support each other**
6. **Help each other**

Having said all that, **it doesn't mean I trust my suppliers blindly.** You still need to have a few control mechanisms in place such as inspection, checking reports and certificates he sends, and not easily accepting price increases. If they are reasonable issues they can be discussed but I will sure do my research on the eligibility of his claim.

CHAPTER 16
HIRING A SOURCING COMPANY

Back in the days when I worked for a Buying Office in Hong Kong I was travelling 10 days of the month scouting new products for Customers. As a Sourcing Company we provided everything the Customer needed for Import so he didn't need to handle everything himself. We earned a small commission (non-profit wholly owned Buying Office) on our orders and made life for our Buyers a lot easier.

This option can be helpful if you do not wish to deal with all the procedures and processes involved. Bear in mind that this can be quite pricy and usually costs 30% on top of the manufacturer's costs. There are hundreds of sourcing companies in China that can help you.

Again, this course is meant for you to skip this part but you can certainly start with small quantities from sourcing companies to test the water. Simply Google "sourcing company in China" and you will get many results.

Here's a shameless self-plug ☺

I've been running my own sourcing company for a little over 2 years now and we have great packages available. Check us out here:

https://importdojo.com/sourcing/

CHAPTER 17
ADVANTAGES AND DISADVANTAGES OF DROP-SHIPPING (E.G. ALIEXPRESS / EBAYEBAY)

AliExpress.com is one of the most used marketplaces in the world. This will be your new favorite channel for B2C and ordering small quantities from suppliers in China. AliExpress.com is part of Alibaba.com, which is also the biggest B2B (business to business) company. They have more than 20 product categories, which include electronics, cell phones, automotive accessories, clothing, jewelry, and other items.

I recommend this option ONLY if you have small order quantities and want to test the water.

Bear in mind that these items are usually stock from the supplier that they sell on Alibaba's marketplace (Aliexpress). Be careful, as many of those items are returned goods from the manufacturer's other customers, faulty items, or over-produced items from another customer's order. In the last case it can easily be an order from some trading company in Thailand and the instruction manual as well as the packaging could be in Thai.

Be sure to check all these details before you place an order to a manufacturer.

In most cases the companies offering the products on Aliexpress are trading companies that buy stock from the manufacturer and sell online.

The prices can be 30-70% more than if you mass-produce with the manufacturer. But again it's a great option if you want to order 5-10 pieces of an item to test the waters.

Here is a rough overview of Aliexpress:

A) Quality of products

You have no way of knowing. Again, these are items that the supplier has in stock. You don't know what's inside and you can't inspect the goods. On a bulk order with a factory you would always install an inspection measurement before shipment. With Aliexpress you have no way of knowing what you are actually getting. If you buy from Aliexpress make sure you use a seller with great reviews and lots of sales. Ask him to send pictures of the product taken out of the gift box, the gift box itself, and the instruction manual that comes with it.

B) Are the Payment Options Safe?

AliExpress.com offers a safe and secure payment option through escrow. Both the buyer and the seller are protected. AliPay (also an Alibaba company) holds the escrow payment. The payment is released to the seller once the transaction is completed. Should there be any disputes or problems, the third party (AliPay in this case) will negotiate between the two parties.

AliPay acts completely neutral and does not favor either party, so you can be sure it is a fair negotiation.

One more benefit of using escrow as payment is you do not have to divulge your credit card number, and in the event that you are not satisfied with the delivered items, you can negotiation the price.

This escrow service is initiated via credit card, Western Union, bank transfer or through other online payment processors. Some suppliers differ from each other on that.

C) Shipment methods

AliExpress.com provides free shipping worldwide. They joined hands with the China Post Mail to provide free shipping worldwide to accommodate smaller orders, especially electronic items. Just recently, AliExpress.com launched Fulfillment by AliExpress, which is designed to accommodate medium orders so that they can have free shipment like bulk orders. This will allow importers at least 30% savings on the shipping costs. However, shipment can be as long as 30-60 days in some cases and there will be no tracking number provided. Shipments could get lost.

AliExpress.com supports DHL, FedEx, TNT, and EMS with the UPS as the most preferred means of shipping goods. These methods deliver product from 2 days up to 7 days, which is good enough considering that we are talking about worldwide deliveries. I recommend using these carriers as there will be tracking, customs help, and obviously you receive goods much faster. Usually the prices for these carriers through AliExpress are quite competitive.

D) Are the prices competitive?

Prices are in general more competitive than if you would buy from your local importer/wholesaler or even online store. The general rule is that the prices are around 30% more than the actual manufacturer's cost. Again, if you have small orders this should still be a good price to add your margin.

E) Example on drop-shipping

There are a lot of drop-shippers from the US on EbayEbay/Amazon that operate under the same principle as Aliexpress. They usually cooperate with a factory in China (e.g., Shenzhen) and buy their over-stock or have the manufacturer produce a certain quantity of a specific product. The factory does the fulfillment while the EbayEbay/Amazon seller does the marketing and sales part.

An Acquaintance of mine, who owns an affiliate marketing website (http://www.cheapcheapcheap.com/) pointed me to a good example and asked me how is it possible that this seller can sell so cheap:

http://www.ebay.com/itm/201253495057

This seller buys from a factory in Shenzhen and the factory has the fulfillment done.

I know for a fact that this item can be bought in bulk quantity for 0.3USD. So they both make a nice profit. And, the EbayEbay selling price is still very cheap.

Now **how can he sell this cheap and include free shipping?**

Many fulfillment centers in China have an amazing deal on logistics with CHINA POST.

Some large fulfillment centers in China ship up to 20,000 pieces of goods a day. Now obviously you will get a great deal for shipping costs with CHINA POST as a fulfillment center. The downside? You as a customer might have to wait for 30-40 days to get your item. Also, there is no tracking or tracing with China Post, so if your parcel gets lost it's gone for good. Many times there will also be customs issues and you may have to pay taxes and duties.

For an item costing only 3USD you can certainly invest 3USD, knowing that your item might get lost.

If you order larger quantities via drop shipping make sure you use a well- known carrier such as DHL/FedEx, etc. You can track and trace the parcel and they will handle customs issues for you too. Money well spent.

Aliexpress Conclusion

A great way to order goods online for small quantities. A few issues here and there that can be solved with the supplier. Quick and easy for starting and testing the waters with the product. The downsides are that you have no way of knowing the quality of the product and that the shipment could get lost (if you use free shipping). Use DHL/FedEx or other big couriers to make sure that your items actually arrive and customs won't hold them up.

CHAPTER 18
PATENTS AND COPIES

Copies

It's very common to find the newest gadget in China at an exhibition but copied and for much less money than the brand sells it for.

Stay away from these!

First of all you could get in trouble when you order a sample and customs picks it up. You could end up paying a fine or worse.

Second, if you do receive the sample and you try to sell it in your store or website, the actual owner of the design can sue you in a lawsuit if he finds out. This could end up being very costly and it's simply not worth it.

There are ways around it such as a slight modification from the patent, but it's still very risky and not worth it.

I remember when Dyson came out with their cool ventilator/fans and vacuum cleaners: http://www.dyson.com/fans-and-heaters/cooling-fans.aspx

A few months later they were everywhere in China. And a year later I recall there were at least three big retailers who bought these copies and had them in their stores. They should have known better. Dyson filed lawsuits, and the retailers had to pay a fine and remove all the items from their shops. Not only were their profits and investment gone, they also had to pay a fine and had their name slammed in the newspapers.

Patents

This goes in hand with the copies. Many designs have patents and again you shouldn't touch these items or try to find a way around the patent. Some suppliers will tell you that they have modified the product so that they don't conflict with the patent. Oh they are so wrong!

If you do buy a modified design and the supplier tells you that there won't be any problems, stay away. He just wants you to place an order to earn a quick buck, but if there is a lawsuit against you I am sure your supplier won't be found anywhere. Read more on patents on Wikipedia:

http://en.wikipedia.org/wiki/Patent

CHAPTER 19
CALCULATE YOUR COSTS

This part makes or breaks your import. It is essential that you calculate all your costs into the product to make sure you can actually turn a profit.

Import duty can be calculated in different ways. I have a rule of thumb myself. I take the buying price from my supplier and add 20-30% on top, regardless on where I export it from (or import in your case). This gives me a rough idea on what my landing price will be. This rule applies to first world locations like the US, Europe, Hong Kong, and Singapore, for example. Many second or third world countries are not so open to importing and put a high percentage of duties and tax on top of import products to protect the local industry.

Many first world places even have 0% duties and tax to encourage importing. This applies especially to "green products" that are very sustainable and help reduce energy or waste. A good example is an LED bulb with 0% tax and duties. Of course you can check in detail through Customs Tariff Numbers (see above) or resources like www.simplyduty.com

Lets look at an example:

My product is a Bluetooth speaker and I would like to import it into the US.

First I calculate my shipping costs. I have the measurements of the product and also of the export cartons through the supplier's quotation. I plan to ship 1,000 pieces.

I go onto http://worldfreightrates.com/ and calculate my shipping costs.

It will cost me roughly 1,200USD.

Now, I go onto www.simplyduty.com (first five checks free)

I input details such as country of manufacture, country of import, product category (this website has a nice and easy to use auto-complete), total product value, my estimated shipping cost, and insurance cost. Shipping cost is the rough estimation of 1000 pieces. Insurance is usually 1% of total product value. I press calculate.

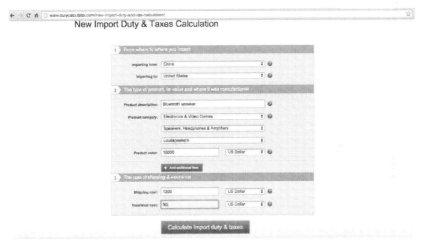

Here we go, I have all costs listed. Wow, only 10% landing costs (excluding shipping costs).

Import duty & taxes calculation result

Here is a breakdown:

Notes on duty and tax rates and compliance:

Bluetooth speaker has an import duty rate of 4.9%. Restrictions may apply for shipping this product with courier or postal companies (some probability).

Packaging and labeling requirements apply to lithium batteries whether they are contained in the equipment or sent separately from the device. Please, contact your courier for more information.

Notes on import taxes due:

For imports with FOB value exceeding 2500USD, a merchandise processing fee of 0.3464% of the FOB value applies, with a minimum of 25USD and maximum of 485USD.

Please note that your shipping provider may add an additional handling fee.

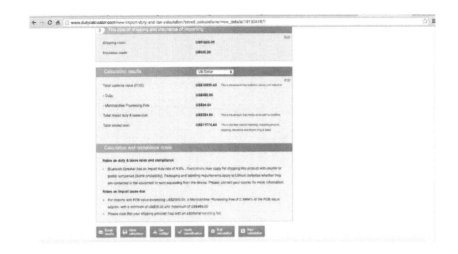

So essentially I have the following import costs:

- 1200USD Shipping
- ~100USD Insurance
- 10,000USD Product value
- 1,774.64USD Customs & duties
- TOTAL: 13,074.64 USD

That leaves me with almost exactly 30% costs on top of all my product costs. Pretty much within my **"rule of thumb of 30%."**

That's **13USD per item** (we have 1,000 pcs). That gives me a great span for margin. I know that the selected Bluetooth speaker is sold for around 49USD.

Obviously I have to calculate my domestic shipping and storage or fulfillment costs on top but I should have a fair margin that I can sell this product with.

I calculate another 8% for fulfillment by Amazon plus another 10% storage and packing costs. I end up with 15.34USD on the item. To be safe I round up to 16USD. That gives me a potential margin of 33USD per item (49USD minus 16USD). Total sales if I sell everything would amount to 49,000USD.

In other words after I have deducted all my costs and investment I have the potential to make **a gross profit of 33,000USD**. I could take that 33,000USD and invest in my next project and build an even larger product portfolio. Not bad I would say.

If you aren't sure about logistic or duty costs you may also contact your logistics provider. We explain this in the next step.

CHAPTER 20
CONTACT A LOGISTICS PROVIDER AND GET A QUOTE

Here are some notes on how to contact your logistics company and what information **YOU** need to provide:

- container volume (your goods in volume, calculated by the supplier)
- estimated order quantity in cartons and units
- number of SKUs (how many different products)
- average dimensions and weights (if you have more than one product)
- labeling requirement (this is covered in labeling and packaging)
- visibility requirement (where do the labels and stickers go)
- delivery points and address (pick up and destination address)
- what material do you provide (labels, boxes, seals?)

If you are unsure of any of the above information ask your supplier to provide this for you. They usually have good experience dealing with logistics companies. Every factory should have a "shipping department."

After you have received the logistics provider's quote you should also ask your factory's logistics provider about a quote, just to compare and make sure you are not getting ripped off and your prices are competitive.

Take the shipping costs into consideration with your customs and tax duties and you have your landing price.

The most viable option of shipment is **sea-shipment**. What does that mean?

There are two different shipments by sea:

FCL – Full Container-Loading

That means that you order a full container from a supplier only packed with your goods. Some items may have a large quantity per container, especially when they are very small.

LCL – Low Container-Loading

You ordered a quantity lower than a full-container-loading and it will be packed with goods from other customers and other suppliers in one container.

When you start off with importing you will probably have a LCL shipment because your quantities will be low. A FCL shipment can easily be a few thousand pieces of your product.

You don't need to arrange anything for the loading and unloading. Your logistics provider will handle this part.

Logistic costs will decrease the more items you order and can fit into a container.

Here is a calculation example:

A 20' container holds 28 cubic-meters. My product (Bluetooth speaker) fits 11,636 pieces into a 20' container. A 20' container to the US typically costs 2,000USD. If I would order different quantities the costs would be as follows:

FCL of my Bluetooth speaker 11,636 pieces. Container cost: 2,000USD

Calculation: 2,000USD / 11,363 pieces = 0.17USD cents per piece of logistic costs (excluding insurance, customs, tax, etc.)

LCL of my Bluetooth speaker say 1,000 pieces. Total CBM of 1,000pcs Bluetooth speaker are roughly 3 CBM. LCL by CBM usually around 100USD

Calculation: 300USD / 1,000 pieces = 0.3USD cents per piece of logistic costs (excluding insurance, customs, tax, etc.)

You see the price per piece halves if I go for FCL. But of course if I start small I will go for the LCL option.

CHAPTER 21
CONTACT A THIRD-PARTY INSPECTION COMPANY TO INSPECT YOUR GOODS

There are several third-party inspection companies in Asia.

Some of the big names are: Buereau Veritas, TUV-SUD, TUV-RHEINLAND, AsiaInspection to name a few. The first three are usually expensive but also very thorough. AsiaInspection is a simple and cost efficient service that should work in the beginning for you.

AsiaInspection has an easy to use Dashboard and Interface. As soon as you register someone will call you to ask if you are in need of any service. They are very helpful and efficient.

Here is what the Dashboard looks like:

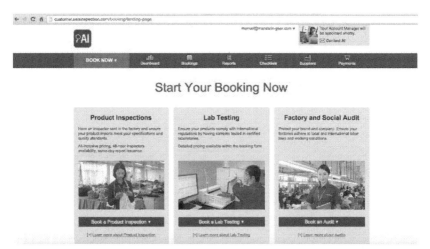

You can book several types of product inspection, send them a sample that you would like to have tested, or have them conduct research and an audit at your supplier.

Types of Product Inspection

- Pre-Shipment Inspection / PSI (Inspect the products after they are fully produced)
- During Production Inspection / DUPRO (Inspect your products during production to make sure everything goes well)
- Initial Production Check / IPC (Inspecting your products at a stage when ~20% of the products are finished)
- Container Loading Check / CLC (Checking proper loading and quantity count during container loading)
- Production Monitoring / PM (Simple monitoring of your products during the production)

Lab Testing:

You can send AsiaInspection your sample, or even better, ask the supplier to send a sample for testing.

What needs to be tested depends on your market and requirements. But they will give you an idea what they can do and what you should have tested.

Factory and Social Audit:

While I recommend that you have the factory audited, many factories are already audited by either Alibaba or some other third-party for other customers.

Simply ask your supplier to send you his latest factory audit report or look on Alibaba. If your supplier is on Alibaba it is likely he has a factory audit that was performed previously. Therefore, you can skip this step if the factory has a valid and positive report.

If you are unsure and your order is large have the factory audited.

Their prices go from 309USD negotiable (full inspection) to 649USD for auditing and more.

If you are purchasing from China for the first time AND the amount is over say 2,000USD it makes sense to have at least a pre-shipment inspection.

This covers basics such as function test, checking the production, and making sure the products are made according to your order-requirements.

You can choose either one or all at the same time, it really depends on how much you trust your supplier and how sensible your product is.

Either way, you can simply do this entire process through the online-booking system. They can also give you a call to discuss details.

Once you have your test or inspection booked and performed they will send you a report on their findings. Depending on the findings you can now decide if you want to place an order to your factory or if the product needs improvements.

As for the other big names such as Bureau Veritas, TUV, SGS, and others I only recommend them if you have business in China in excess of 500,000USD. They are usually more thorough, with more detailed reports and so on. But they also come with a high price tag.

CHAPTER 22
CREATE AN INTERNAL FORM TO FOLLOW UP YOUR ORDER

I recommend once your order is placed that you have administrative files for yourself to monitor the order. This could simply be a checklist in Word or Excel.

Here is what it could look like. You can copy sections or make your own checklist based on this.

Installation		CHECKLIST FOR		
Order number:		Date issued:		
PI #:		Order issued by:		
Supplier:				
Manufacturer:				
Latest shipment date:				
Product description / model no. :				
TOTAL VALUE		$0.00		
			Needed	Finished
SAMPLE REFUND	Supplier sample refund	YES		
Documents:	PVI	yes	yes	
	P/O + L/C	yes/no	yes/no	
		yes		
Labies!		yes		
Packing:	Private label	no		
	Instruction Manual	yes		
	Supplier packaging	no		
	Language	yes		
	Bar code	yes		
	Shipping marks	yes		
Certificates	GS + test report + CDF	yes		
	EMC + test report + CDF	no		
	CE for EMC + test report	yes		
	EC DOC (TMX format)	yes		
	EN71	no		
	EMC cert./ COC for C.C.	yes		
	Others	yes		
Inspection	PSI	no		
	Factory Audit	yes		
	Others	yes		
	Others	no		
Shipment:	Shipping documents	yes		
No of shipment	Destination	Cont.	Ship date	
Forwarder				
Short shipment :			Total	

CHAPTER 23
THINGS YOU SHOULD DO BEFORE PLACING AN ORDER

So you have evaluated your suppliers, calculated your costs, reviewed the sample, researched the market, and you are ready to place an order?

Follow this simple guide to make sure you cover everything:

- Payment terms with your supplier are clear and negotiated
- Delivery time and method is clear and discussed with the supplier
- Your forwarder is informed and standing by for shipment
- Inspection company has been contacted/briefed and is standing by
- Your warehouse is ready to receive the goods
- Customs/tax and license issues have been clarified with your government
- A form has been created for your reference to follow up on the order
- Holidays in China have been considered (CNY, Tsueng Mun Festival, etc.)

CHAPTER 24
PACKING AND LABELING

When sending an order you should also include any labels or numbers that you wish to have printed on the gift-box, product, or export cartons. Your supplier should be asking you (once you place your order) about the labeling requirements. These are examples:

Specific marking and labeling is used to facilitate the following issues:

- Meet legal shipping regulations
- Ensure proper handling
- Conceal the identity of the contents
- Help receivers identify shipments and forwarding requirements
- Insure compliance with environmental and safety standards

You as the buyer need to specify (with the help of the supplier) which export marks should appear on your cargo for easy identification. Products can require many markings for shipment. For example, exporters need to put the following markings on cartons to be shipped:

- Shipper's mark
- Country of origin (CHINA)
- Weight (in pounds and in kilograms)
- Number of packages and size of cases (in inches and centimeters)
- Handling marks (international pictorial symbols)

- Safety markings such as "This Side Up" (in English and in the language of the country of destination)
- Port of entry
- Product description (a short description is sufficient and should be in the language of the destination country)

Export carton markings usually look like this:

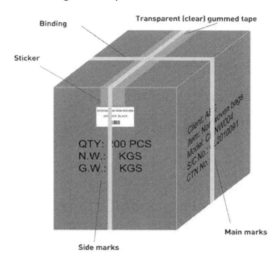

The export carton marks should clearly be stated on your PO (order form) and from the supplier's side on his packing list or invoice. It could look like this:

PORT OF SHIPMENT: NINGBO, CHINA	PORT OF DESCHARGE: BREMERHAVEN	PORT OF DELIVERY: VIENNA, AUSTRIA				
MARKS & NOS.	DESCRIPTION	QUANTITY	PACKAGES	WEIGHT		MEASUREMENT
				GROSS	NET	
	FLUORESCENT LIGHT	PCS	CNTS	KGS	KGS	M³
WARENIMPORT & HANDELS GMBH P.O. NO. ART. NO. BMX NO. EAN NO. FEUCHTRAUMLEUCHTE MENGE: VIENNA VIA HAMBURG/BREMERHAV EN CARTON NO.	ITEM NO. LG236A. BMX NO. 3334539. BARCODE NO. 9004181211225. BAUMAX ARTICLE NO.3334539. 48PCS/CARTON, CARTON SIZE:129.70X75.30X83.00CM	3888	81	10935.00	9315.00	65.66
	TOTAL:	3888	81	10935.00	9315.00	65.66

Markings should appear on three faces of the cargo, preferably on the top and on the two ends or the two sides.

Customs regulations regarding freight labeling are strictly enforced. For example, many countries require that the country of origin be clearly labeled on each imported package. Most freight forwarders and export packing specialists can supply the necessary information regarding specific regulations.

Example of labels on gift boxes depending on where you sell:

Labels on products:

Some products require labels on the product itself with basic information. These are called rating labels. In textiles for example it's the little tag that's in the back. Again, your supplier should have examples or give you these labels:

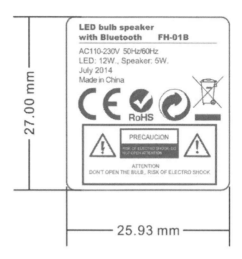

Here is what a typical rating label looks like:

I provide simple labels and formats in this course.

http://importdojo.com/importdojo-masterclass/

If you are unsure about the required labeling speak with your supplier at the forwarding/logistics company. They usually know what goes where.

CHAPTER 25
MINIMUM ORDER QUANTITIES (MOQ)

Most suppliers give you an incredibly high amount for an MOQ. Most of the time this is fairly negotiable. Say for example a supplier gives you a MOQ of 1,000 pieces, and that is his desired quantity to start production.

There are ways around this. If, for example, you are not in need of a color gift box but would rather have a white box the quantities tumble. Most suppliers will agree to produce 200 pieces for a white box.

So why the 1,000 pieces? For one, 1,000pcs is usually the minimum order quantity for colored or private label gift boxes. That's a fact and some printing factories actually require more than 1,000pcs.

If you want, say, 300pcs of an item and a color box you may ask the factory if they can still print the color box if you are willing to pay a higher price for the printing of the gift box.

If you don't need a gift box but you want some label or logo on the box you can ask them to put stickers on it. Stickers usually cost a few cents and can be printed easily.

CHAPTER 26
NEGOTIATION

It is a given that once you place your order you negotiate the price.

No matter if you are below the supplier's MOQ or not. You are now ready to place the order and you let the supplier know your terms.

Use the price that you were originally quoted and decrease it by 20%. Give this target price to the factory and let him know you would like to order with your (20% reduced) price. In many cases the supplier may not agree to your new target price but he may reduce it another 5%.

In 80% of the cases he will give you a further reduction on his original quoted price, unless your quantity is really very low.

Also mention to him that this will be the first trial order and that if it is successful larger orders will follow.

Once your price is negotiated you are ready to send your PO.

This could be an informal text in an email with all details or a Word/PDF file that you have created. We will supply a blank Proforma Order in this course.

CHAPTER 27
PAYMENT OPTIONS

If you are buying through Alibaba use the escrow service. If you have met the supplier outside of Alibaba I recommend either going with a letter of credit (L/C at sight) or with a 20-30% down payment by telegraphic transfer (TT).

My recommendation for a first-time importer would be TT payment with a 30% down payment, and the rest after you have received the copy of the shipment documents. This option is generally safe and should be used for any amount from 1,000-20,000USD.

If you have a large order above 20,000USD I recommend the option L/C.

This is safe for both sides as you only pay once the supplier has shipped all goods. On the other hand a supplier can use the copy of your L/C draft (the bank will send you this draft) to purchase raw material so he can get going and has his production costs covered. Once you release the shipment the bank will release the funds from the L/C to the supplier's bank.

For smaller amounts I would go with either PayPal or Western Union.

If in doubt about your supplier's credibility or if he insists on 100% upfront payment STAY AWAY. It is not a good sign if he wants payment upfront. He may be in financial trouble or he might end up scamming you out of your money. Again, any supplier will agree with 30% down payment or L/C.

CHAPTER 28
PLACING THE ORDER - THE ESSENTIALS

You are ready to place the order. Make sure all details in previous sections are clear.

- Inform the supplier within your order that you will perform an inspection. The costs are on you but if any re-work is necessary another inspection will be on his account.
- Price and article number (including any color reference)
- Shipment Date
- Payment Terms
- Inspection Date
- Logistics Provider
- If possible attach a product picture
- Instruction on labels, markings on the carton
- Instructions for Destination Address (your address)
- Export carton markings
- Rating labels

Place your order and wait for the supplier's confirmation or PI (pro-forma invoice)

Pay attention to public holidays in China. These can seriously affect your order and shipment. Here are seven main holidays in China where most of the factories are off (excerpt from Wikipedia):

Date	English name	Pinyin	Dates (2014) [2]
January 1	New Year	Yuándàn	Wed 1 January
1st day of 1st lunar month	Chinese New Year[3]	Chūnjié	Fri 31 January - Thu 6 February[4]
5th solar term (April 4 or April 5)	Qingming Festival	Qīngmíng jié	Mon 7 April[5]
May 1	Labour Day	Láodòng jié	Thu 1-Sat 3 May[6]
5th day of 5th lunar month	Dragon Boat Festival	Duānwǔ jié	Mon 2 June [7]
15th day of 8th lunar month	Mid-Autumn Festival	Zhōngqiū jié	Mon 8 September[7]
October 1	National Day	Guóqìng jié	Wed 1-Tue 7 October[8]

The period with most holidays is the Chinese New Year. Some factories close up to 4 weeks, which means that your order is in a long queue before and after the Chinese New Year. Try to ship goods out before Chinese New Year.

The general lead-time for shipment from the day of order placement, to shipping, to goods arriving at your warehouse is around 90 days.

Here is a breakdown on why:

- Order placement and administrative clarification (labels, packaging, etc.): 5 days
- Purchase of raw material: 20-30 days
- Arrangement of production: 10 days
- Start of production until shipment: 5-10 days
- Shipment (goods at sea): 30 days
- Customs clearance and transport to warehouse: 5-10 days

Keep this in mind when planning promotions or sales.

CHAPTER 29
RECEIVING YOUR PI (PRO-FORMA INVOICE)

The supplier should send you his invoice now.

Pay attention to all details especially the following:

- Unit price
- Quantity
- Payment Terms
- Shipment
- Order number

Here is an example of what an invoice might look like:

NINGBO HOMELITE IMP.& EXP.CO.,LTD.
Room 2318 NO. 666 Jinyu Rd, Ningbo, China.
TEL: +86-574-87166415   FAX: +86-574-87166495

COMMERCIAL INVOICE

BUYER:			INVOICE NO. :		DATE:
BAUMAX IMPORT & LOGISTIK GMBH			HT12029		30-Jul-12
AUFELDSTRASSE 17-23, A-3400 KLOSTERNEUBURG,			BAUMAX ORDER NO. :		
AUSTRIA/EUROPE			950325		
PORT OF SHIPMENT:	PORT OF DESCHARGE:		PORT OF DELIVERY:		
NINGBO, CHINA	BREMERHAVEN		VIENNA, AUSTRIA		
MARKS & NOS.	DESCRIPTION		QUANTITY	UNIT PRICE FOR NINGBO	AMOUNT
	FLUORESCENT LIGHT		PCS	US$	US$
WARENIMPORT & HANDELS GMBH P.O. NO. ART. NO. BMX NO. EAN NO. FEUCHTRAUMLEUCHTE MENGE: VIENNA VIA HAMBURG/BREMERHAVEN CARTON NO.	ITEM NO. LG236A. BMX NO. 3334539. BARCODE NO.9004181211225. BAUMAX ARTICLE NO.3334539. 48PCS/CARTON		4800	12.18	58464.00
	ITEM NO. LG258A. BMX NO.10140673.BARCODE NO.9004181211232. BAUMAX ARTICLE NO.10140673. 4PCS/CARTON		500	14.96	7480.00
	TOTAL		5300		65,944.00

SAY TOTAL U.S.DOLLAR SIXTY FIVE THOUSAND NINE HUNDRED AND FORTY FOUR ONLY.

ALL OTHER DETAILS AS PER ORDER NO. 950325

NUMBER OF BAUMAX IMPORT & LOGISTIC GMBH ORDER: 950325

EACH PIECE HAS AN EAN CODE (MADE IN CHINA), MULTILANGUAGE

DESCRIPTION AND IMPORTER INFORMATION AND GREEN DOT LOGO OUTSIDE

EACH EXPORT CARTON HAVE BEEN MARKED WITH BAUMAX ORDER NO., BAUMAX ARTICLE NO. AND EAN-BARCODE

You can sign back the PI if you want but I wouldn't recommend it. Have your own Purchase Order be signed by the supplier (including your purchase terms)

CHAPTER 30
MONITORING YOUR ORDER

This is VITAL. You cannot just place the order and sit back and relax.

Make sure you keep in communication with the supplier. It doesn't need to be on a daily basis but it wouldn't hurt to check on the status once a week, especially if you are in the process of arranging the inspection or shipment date with your inspection company/logistics provider.

Unfortunately, the suppliers get a lot of orders so some smaller orders may be given less priority. Keep reminding him of the deadlines that you have set out.

It is common that a few parts of the order, such as the shipping mark on the export carton, packaging, etc., are discussed AFTER order placement.

That doesn't mean you don't need to prepare for everything on your side before order placement. But it will save you time having the instructions for the supplier ready before order placement.

It wouldn't make much sense to flood the supplier at order placement with all information, but the essentials need to be covered. Essentials are mentioned in the previous chapter.

Make yourself a **CHECKLIST** (Iprovide a simple check-list under http://importdojo.com/importdojo-masterclass/

Mark things complete or chase the supplier when things are dangling in the air. See above in Chapter 22 for an example of a check-list.

CHAPTER 31
ARRANGING THE INSPECTION

There are several third-party inspection companies in Asia.

Some of the big names are: Buereau Veritas, TUV-SUD, TUV-RHEINLAND, and AsiaInspection to name a few. The first three are usually expensive but also very thorough. AsiaInspection is a simple and cost efficient service that should work in the beginning for you.

Register on their website and simply create an order with them. You can fill out all the details or even better ask your supplier to send them a sample. With this sample they will later go to the factory on the inspection date and compare the actual sample with the production units.

Once the inspection is completed they will send you an inspection report. Based on this report you can either:

- Release the shipment to the supplier
- Ask the supplier to re-work the goods according to your agreed terms and fix problems found during the inspection

Only when you are entirely satisfied should you release the shipment. In most cases there will be minor findings, such as scratches, dents, or packaging issues. If this doesn't bother you then release. If there are major problems like faulty wires or wrong colors, ask your supplier to re-work the goods.

Trust me, he will re-work, as he is still waiting to get the full payment. Remember, NEVER pay everything up front.

Once everything is as it should be you can give your logistics provider the order to pick up the goods and send them to the port.

Here are a few pages on what an inspection report might look like:

Inspection Report （PSI）

O-cn-1139153

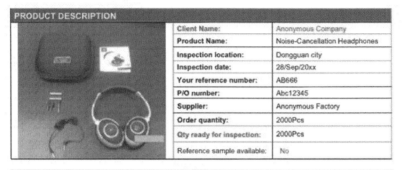

PRODUCT DESCRIPTION	
Client Name:	Anonymous Company
Product Name:	Noise-Cancellation Headphones
Inspection location:	Dongguan city
Inspection date:	28/Sep/20xx
Your reference number:	AB666
P/O number:	Abc12345
Supplier:	Anonymous Factory
Order quantity:	2000Pcs
Qty ready for inspection:	2000Pcs
Reference sample available:	No

OVERALL INSPECTION RESULT: Failed
(Client has the final decision to Reject or Approve)

INSPECTION RESULT SUMMARY

	Result	Findings/Remarks		
			CRITICAL	MAJOR	MINOR
WORKMANSHIP (defectives list)	Within AQL	Found	0	2	4
		Max	0	3	7
		Checked	125	125	125

Most serious defects found:

TESTS	Passed	
QUANTITY	OK	
ARTWORKS	Not OK	Artwork of gift box was different from client's spec
SHIPPING MARKS	N/A	

OTHER REMARKS

1. Artwork of the gift box was different from client's spec;
2. No approved sample for inspection reference.
3. Repacked 125pcs after inspection.

102

2. Product appearance

Expected Result	Result	Actual Finding / Comments
	N/A	Referred to "your product" part

3. Color

Expected Result	Result	Actual Finding / Comments
Black--	OK	
		Pantone Code: Close to black C
Silver--	OK	
		Pantone Code: Close to 877C

4. Artwork

Logo Reference	Result	Production sample vs. Approval sample
DEFECTIVE LOGO IF ANY Client's comments: PLEASE SEE FILES ATTACHED	N/A	Referred to pictures below

You are of course entitled to skip this process, but it is highly recommended, especially for first-timers and for order amounts above 2,000USD.

CHAPTER 32
LOGISTICS - GETTING YOUR ORDER

You have prearranged with your own or the supplier's logistics provider for pick-up and delivery. Here are your options on forms of delivery.

SEA SHIPMENT

The supplier has released the goods and sent the shipping documents to your logistics provider. It's now time to contact your logistics provider to arrange the shipment.

For most cases these are the documents that you need to provide to your logistics company:

For example, in the US:

The US does not require an import license for most items. You need:

- Customs Bond
- Customs Broker
- ISF / HBL / Bill of Landing
- Packing List
- Commercial Invoice w/ Harmonized Tariff Codes
- Shipment advice

For example, in Europe:

- Commercial Invoice
- Packing List
- Certificate of Origin (sometimes)

- Bill of Lading
- Declaration of Conformity (EC-DOC)
- Shipment Advice

As previously mentioned, you should arrange details before placing an order to the factory so that you know the logistics provider has space for you on the container ship for your desired shipment date.

Your logistics provider will guide you through all necessary steps and will advise you when your order will be received at the destination.

The general lead-time for shipment from the factory to your warehouse is around 35-40 days. Keep this in mind when planning promotions or sales.

I also provide a few examples of shipping documents under

http://importdojo.com/importdojo-masterclass/

Time to wait for your goods.

AIR-SHIPMENT

Sometimes it makes sense to air-ship the whole lot, but only if your order is not large in terms of quantity and weight. Prices can quickly go up twenty-fold compared to sea-shipment.

Sure, you get your goods probably within a week but you might end up losing all your profit margin on the logistics.

Contact your provider on this option. He will guide you through all necessary documentation.

Shipping by air via mail can be another option. But remember that parcels might get lost due to no-tracking availability and long shipping times. See more under the chapter "ALIEXPRESS."

Time to wait for your goods.

CHAPTER 33
RECEIVING YOUR ORDER

Once you have paid all necessary customs taxes and duties your order should be received within your warehouse/facility.

Upon receipt, check the contents of all goods. If you ordered a large amount of pieces this should be done professionally by a fulfillment center/company.

Check the content of goods and open a few boxes to make sure you received the right items.

Your products are ready to sell!

CHAPTER 34
CLAIMS AND COMPENSATION

Ok, so your received goods are damaged, the wrong plug is attached, or the goods are returned from your customer for not functioning or other reasons.

This is a bit tricky.

I use this following tactic only when it's absolutely the manufacturer's fault. If I also made a mistake perhaps on the order sheet or not having stated something clearly I will go mild on him and try to settle for compensation rather than a claim.

Collect all information on returned or damaged items. Document with photos, emails, and reports from your customers.

Start by calculating your loss incurred due to broken/damaged items and incurred loss due to loss of sales. Take this desired figure and add 20%.

Why 20%? Because the supplier will probably only offer you 50% of your total claim in his first response. Hopefully you can settle on the 100% (without your fictitious 20%)

Send a combined and detailed report to the supplier and state your claim with the desired amount.

If it is a new supplier he will probably try to wriggle himself out.

But if you have actual proof there is nothing he can do – but he will try to pay as little of the claim as possible.

In many cases the supplier will offer a discount on your next order. This may be acceptable if you plan on reordering and the supplier is usually reliable with your other orders/shipments.

If you do not plan on reordering from this factory you may as well demand compensation right away. I would not go as far as to threaten the supplier, but daily calls and emails will definitely help if he is stubborn on compensation.

Eventually, you will hopefully settle for the actual desired amount.

Another option is, if you have actually done an **inspection by a third party** and the report of this inspection shows no problems on the production or that particular problem you can actually claim money from the **third-party.** But you will need substantial proof, same as with the supplier. This can be done in addition to the claim to the factory to get the maximum compensation for your occurred loss.

There are also a few legal options if you are within your rights. You might want to get in touch with an expat lawyer within China or a lawyer based in your home country.

Some suppliers have product liability insurance (http://en.wikipedia.org/ wiki/Product_liability), which covers the loss due to a a problem with their products.

If you are importing large quantities regularly I also recommend you look into this with your trusted insurance company. There are a few within China/Hong Kong that provide this service if you don't find anything within your home country. For example, HSBC ,which is the largest bank within Asia that most suppliers use.

CHAPTER 35
SELLING YOUR PRODUCTS (EBAY / AMAZON)

So you received your goods, everything went well, and you are ready to sell.

A very popular way of selling your goods from China these days is FBA (Fulfillment by Amazon) or fulfillment centers that cater to eBay or any online store that you sell on (e.g., Shopify).

I have also created several online course in June 2015 / April 2016 & April 2017 that cover the complete process. From sourcing in China to selling professionally on Amazon to building an actual brand.

Check it out here: https://importdojo.com/courses/

Here's a brief overview on my 3 courses:

COURSE 1) The ImportDojo Masterclass

The Amazon Case Study

Private labeling a product in China and shipping it to Amazon.

Do you still worry about your importing business sometimes? Wouldn't it be nice to have it run like you have been running it for a long long time already?

Of course it would. Business feels great once routine settles in. This is exactly the point I want to get you to and with this case study you can see a complete product launch that starts from finding the right product, the right supplier and shipping it to Amazon, promoting and selling it.

Every little step is documented with a video (over 50 video tutorials) that shows my screen and you can even listen to me talking to suppliers.

Best thing about this, I'm using my own money and will try a lot of different things so you can see what works and what doesn't and learn all this without running your own trial and error experiments.

If you don't sell yet, simply sit back and watch the whole process and you can leave all your worries and anxiety behind.

Feel confident to launch your own business and become financially independent or simply make your existing import business more efficient. This is it! Can't be easier!

The results of my case study where I went from ZERO to 7,000US$ within 7 days of my launch can be found here:

http://importdojo.com/case-study-how-i-went-from-zero-to-7000us-in-10-days-in-one-of-the-most-competitive-amazon-niches/

Whats more, after 6 months I reached the number 1 Bestseller rank in this super competitive category.

Check it out here: http://importdojo.com/importdojo-masterclass/

COURSE 2: Certificates and requirements when importing from China to the US & Europe

http://importdojo.com/module/import-dojo-certification/

Product Safety Road Map for importing products and knowing regulations and requirements to ensure compliance with all mandatory safety standards & labeling requirements.

Ever wondered what your product needs in terms of certification when importing in your home country? This course explains in detail and takes out all the guesswork.

To give you a basic understanding of requirements and regulations out there. Also to give you actionable PDF"s (30+) that you can send to your supplier.

For each product category you'll get a testing plan that testing laboratories usually charge 50-150$ per product.

This is the ONLY course of its kind on the internet. Approx 7 hours of content, 30+ actionable PDF's and templates to help succeed.

COURSE 3: ImportDojo Brand Evolution

Overview of Chapters here:
http://importdojo.com/module/import-dojo-brand-evolution/

Competition has increased a lot and now only the fittest will survive. Amazon is a great platform to get started but it is not the only sales channel out there.

If you truly want to build a brand and beat the competition you need to branch out into other sales channels including other Amazon marketplaces. On top of that, most importers don't even know that they have to meet certain country regulations. Governments, retailers and eCommerce channels like Amazon will become stricter and stricter.

You need to stay ahead and be fully prepared of what's to come. Simply buying a product in China and putting it on Amazon won't guarantee your survival anymore! You'll want to be better than the rest out there and bring your business to the next level.

111

Most courses out there only focus on a specific strategy which might not be viable anymore. What we offer is something no one else does. We looked at all parts of building a business and a brand not just on Amazon but many other sales channels. You need to look at long term strategies. Amazon can close your account any day without prior warning. You'll want several income streams and have ultimate control in every part of your business. We'll show you how you can build trust with your customers and turn this into a powerful tool to increase sales.

From pricing and inventory, to closing deals with large retailers that will help exposing your brand to new audiences, this course is all about giving you the confidence to expand your business further. Amazon is still the most popular sales channel, and selling on there will always be viable and it will grow even more in the future. However, the point is to diversify and secure your survival.

Even if you are already selling a few products on Amazon - Don't stop there! Your products might sell well on other channels too. Imagine if you already have a lot of products on Amazon, you can take those same exact products and expand into other sales channels - the opportunities are endless! This course will stand the test of time because it looks at the bigger picture of an Ecommerce business and does not focus on just one sales channel.

So let me guide through some of the things you will learn in this course:

Choosing a Product

Even if you're an established seller, chances are you're still looking at new products to sell right now! This module will help you devise a strategy to launch great products - each and every time! But that's not all, a unique brand is ultimately more valuable.

That's why we have dedicated a complete section on patents and how to analyze your competition effectively. Remember, generic products are not working anymore and if you truly want to innovate, you need to have Intellectual Property unique to your brand. We'll also show you in a unique and foolproof way, how to find innovative products.

Business Incorporation

Having a strong legal structure behind your business will be vital for your success. For this reason, we have researched the best countries in the world to incorporate your business. The main goal of this module is making your business more attractive to investors, especially if you want to sell your business down the road.

A strong business is also a profitable one! You might agree with us that in this business, fees can really kill your profit margins. However, we have got you covered in our business banking section. We have done extensive research on the best business bank accounts, currency exchange and transfer accounts to make sure your brand saves money and becomes more profitable.

Social Media

Knowing your target audience will be essential if you want to build a raving fan base that purchases every product you launch. When it comes to building audiences in your market, there is no better way than having a social media strategy. We have asked around in groups launched questionnaires and polls and the issue most people have these days is actually not sourcing or PPC or inventory management -

but how to launch a product. I truly believe Influencer marketing and having a strong social media presence will be your KEY tool for the years to come when launching products. Influencer marketing is exploding right now and it will be the only way to get your product off the ground!

In this module, we will guide you step by step through all the social media platforms and how you can successfully build an audience behind your brand. Having a social media strategy in place is not only vital to get your brand noticed, but also to drive sales and get market share from your competition. Building social media presence is not a sprint but a marathon. I am not going to lie, it will take time to build an audience, but if you start now, you'll have the most powerful tool on the market.

The best part is that we will not only give you a clear strategy on how you can drive insane amounts of traffic to your Amazon listing, but also to your website. Younger audiences are also moving away from traditional sales channels like retail, and they are shopping on social media. After going through this module, you will have a platform where you can connect with your customers and showcase your products freely.

Retail

I've been in retail for over 18 years now and that's where I actually started out. I've built a 7-figure retail business before even moving onto Amazon. I'll discuss retail in detail and how you can reach out to retailers. I'll show you how I find retailers in a foolproof way. I'll show you how I prepare marketing materials that you can send to retailers and how you can follow up and push for sales.

You'll also learn how to price your products to retailers and which contracts you need to prepare beforehand when you work with them. I've made profits as big as 50,000$ with retailers in one day and I will show you how you can do it too.

Certifications

Have you ever wondered what you need to meet legally when importing from China. Are you worried about test reports, customs and what national laws and standards you need to meet when you buy a product from China? Are you worried that your product might get seized at customs? Not sure what test reports you need when you import something? Then this is for you. Get a practical roadmap to ensure compliance with all mandatory safety standards & labelling requirements for Europe and North America.

I'll walk you through all major regulations and requirements when importing to Europe and the US such as CE, RoHS, FDA, FCC or REACH. You'll understand what you need to meet legally as well what your supplier needs to fulfill for you. Have you ever looked up a regulation and understood only half of what you need to do? Have you ever contacted a test laboratory and been quoted thousands of dollars in testing costs? Did you ever wonder how you can make your product compliant but don't know where to save money? I've made it very easy for you. I'll explain everything in laymen's terms and hand you tools and resources that will help you navigate through all the mazes of regulations and standards.

This is just a brief overview of the entire course. There are many other modules that will help build and elevate your brand. Our ultimate goal with this course to is help you build a business that is stronger, profitable and more successful than your competitors. After going through our course, you will have learned how to take control over your business and build a brand loved by its customers, in any market you plan to sell.

Join me today and learn how to start a global brand & build an ecommerce empire.

If you have any question about the courses, simply email me at: mail@importdojo.com

I also provide sourcing services for "first-timers" or even experienced buyers who would like to take their import business to the next step. Please contact us at mail@importdojo.com or through my website:

http://importdojo.com/sourcing/

PART 2

THE IMPORT BIBLE – PROFESSIONAL EDITION

ABOUT THIS PART

This part of the eBook is aimed at entrepreneurs who have already tested the waters of importing from China through Alibaba, exhibitions, contacts and more. If you have already started to import goods from China this course will take you to the next level.

I outline the most important steps to keep your business growing, what to avoid when importing from China, how to communicate with suppliers on a daily basis, what to expect when in China, visiting exhibitions and how to arrange factory meetings.

I tell you about the most important processes and explain them in detail.

Let me teach you how I negotiated contracts, battled price increases, got bonus payments for my buyers in the amount of 100,000USD in a day and how I got a supplier to air-ship goods on his account for 50,000USD.

I will break it down to you as simply as I can with lots of practical examples on "how-to."

I will dedicate a section on how to implement your PL (private label) from the beginning to actually selling it. I give you an example on how I did it.

Again, as in the first part of this eBook there will be sections that may or may not apply to you. I recommend reading them anyway.

PART 2
THE IMPORT BIBLE – PROFESSIONAL GUIDE

CHAPTER 1
RE-ORDERS AND WHAT TO KEEP IN MIND

Once you see your stock dwindle because your item has sold well you should consider re-ordering from the supplier.

Remember that from order placement until arrival of goods it can take up to 90 days (for larger quantities and sea-shipment).

The good news is that re-ordering usually takes half the time. The reason for this is because the supplier has all your details and order specifications on hand.

So unless you would like to have something changed this is a fairly simple process.

If your item sells very well you should also consider increasing **the order quantity**. If your item has not sold well but you need it anyway then order the same quantity or consider decreasing it by 20-30%.

You should also check on **any modifications** you wish to give the supplier. You should know your modifications based on your customers' feedback. This could include: different color options, longer cables and cords, packaging or instruction manual changes and more. It may be that you will face a price increase but unless there is any change in material or greater effort for the supplier this can be negotiated.

You will also want to **re-negotiate** the price of your re-order. Even if the quantity changes or you request a modification of the product, you should at least try. The simplest reason you can give to justify this to the supplier is because you are re-ordering and giving the supplier more business. He will be very happy to discuss the price if you are re-ordering. At the very least, you should negotiate the last price. This can be difficult if the last order took place more than a year ago, but, again, the supplier should be open to discussions about price.

Once you are ready to place a re-order, send an email to your supplier and issue yourself a new order follow-up checklist. (See the Import Bible and document support section under www.importdojo.com.)

Process of re-ordering:

- **Calculate the stock you have and how long you have until the stock will be sold out**
- **Take shipment times into consideration**
- **Request a modification of the product (if applicable)**
- **Re-negotiate the price**
- **Follow the checklist of your previous order**

After you have confirmed the details with your supplier you can start the whole process from the beginning. It should be a lot easier for you now to remember the steps. If you have trouble remembering, follow your checklist or look up the process in the *Import Bible*.

CHAPTER 2
THE CHINESE NEW YEAR & WHAT IT MEANS FOR YOUR BUSINESS

Wikipedia excerpt:

Chinese New Year celebrations traditionally run from Chinese New Year's Eve, the last day of the last month of the Chinese calendar, to the Lantern Festival on the 15th day of the first month, making the festival the longest in the Chinese calendar. The first day of the New Year falls between January 21 and February 20.

The Chinese New Year is traditionally a time to celebrate with family and friends. Many workers will travel to their hometown during that time. Some workers come from far away provinces within China so they usually will be gone for at least 2 weeks. Why is this? Some rural areas in China do not have much manufacturing industries or employment opportunities, so people need to travel far to manufacturing areas for work. These workers will usually stay all year with the factory and then leave for 2 weeks during Chinese New Year to return to their hometowns.

Factories

What does that mean for your business? Factories will be closed for up to 3 weeks!

The actual public holidays are usually only 7 days (depending on the province) but factories take this opportunity to send their workers home, as this will be the only annual leave most workers have all year. The factory will most likely not give staff/workers any additional holidays during the year.

Staff/workers

Unfortunately for factories, many workers do not return to the factory after the holidays. The percentage of workers not returning can be up to 50% in some cases.

This leaves factories in a troubled spot. Not only have they been closed for weeks and losing business but now they **can't fulfill orders** from clients because workers are scarce.

This can result in long production times for you after the Chinese New Year.

It's also difficult to reach many factories during the Chinese New Year. Sometimes it's not clear how long they will be closed and who will return to answer your emails/phone calls. Make sure that you ask your factory/supplier for details on their Chinese New Year operation hours.

To battle this problem many factories have great incentives in place, such as bonuses, educational programs, free dormitories or lunch within the factory, which makes workers return.

As for regular staff of the factory this shouldn't be a big issue for you.

Most staff has a higher salary than workers (sometimes it can be the opposite), which will include your sales contact at the factory. They usually enjoy more benefits than workers, such as health insurance, bonuses or provided accommodations.

Logistics

Since the factories are closed, most of the logistics companies will also close, but those will most likely only close for the official days of the public holidays.

Be aware that many companies try to ship out their orders before Chinese New Year. This is a very busy season for all parties involved. Logistic companies will also charge you higher than usual rates during this period. Many vessels will be fully booked, so make sure that you reserve and book your space when you have an upcoming shipment.

CHAPTER 3
STAYING IN TOUCH

Insisting on new products

Why? Because you also live off the ideas and developments of your factory.

Staying in touch with your supplier/factory is very important to your product development process. You need to be ahead of the industry and competition and you need to provide new ideas and trends to your customers.

Factories don't offer you new products because they are under-staffed and sales people have no time to proactively offer you new products, or they simply do not have the motivation or proper staff for sales and business development.

I remember 10 years ago I always needed to chase my suppliers to send me new material that I could offer buyers. I mean, it's so obvious – the more they send and promote their items the more people will buy. It was frustrating. But things have changed a bit since then and now most factories train their sales staff to offer new items proactively.

Nonetheless, make sure that you send your supplier a monthly or bi-monthly email to check if he has any new product ideas. If he doesn't then give him input on your ideas and he may be willing to develop the product for you.

How to maintain supplier relationships

Keep in touch! No matter if you have product inquires, orders or un-related things to discuss with the supplier, the better the relationship with your supplier the more you benefit.

I have 1 or 2 suppliers that I **talk to on a weekly basis**. Sometimes he calls me or vice versa and we chat about the newest developments within our industry.

You can ask each other questions on anything really. It is so incredibly valuable to have a good contact within the industry in China. I often ask my contact things outside business, like, "have you heard of this factory closing" or "do you know who produces this item for Wal-Mart/Apple etc."

Because of my contacts, sometimes I know when my competitor's factory will close before he himself knows.

Your contact can give you **valuable information** that can put you ahead of the competition.

Factory bosses often get together and talk over tea or Mao Tai (a not so delicious rice liquor) about the newest gossip. Their customers' secrets quickly spread within China.

Even bosses that are in competition with each other will be friends and may even refer customers to each other.

Communication

Obviously there is email, but I prefer to call my supplier and quickly have a talk instead of writing a lengthy email and waiting for days for an answer. A phone call can be quick and your problems or questions solved within a few minutes.

I often use Skype, since calls via Skype are very cheap no matter where you are based.

I also use QQ or We Chat, the latter of which is preferred by most Chinese. If I am not mistaken it's not possible to download WhatsApp within China, so most people don't have it. You might as well download QQ or We Chat already so you can chat via messenger to your supplier in China.

When it comes to talking about your orders always be polite and stick to the topics. State the facts and don't let it become personal. Threatening your supplier won't get you any further. You need to remain professional and focus on the task you wish to accomplish.

And the way to accomplish this is to pragmatically approach the supplier. Giving him the idea that when he helps you it will also benefit him is a much better approach than forcing him to do something for you. I like to call that **"Inception,"** from the movie with Leo diCaprio.

INCEPTION

For example, if you sell to retailers or wholesalers in your country and some of them request a specific certification or factory standard, this will cost the factory some money.

I remember this one customer from Germany. They required every new factory to have BSCI standard. (Business Social Compliance Initiative to establish certain social standards for workers in factories.)

This audit and standards cost roughly 8,000USD. To implement these standards it usually means than just the third party auditor cost but also upgrades on certain things in the factory. It involves mostly work on the factory's side, mainly to improve the factory to a higher social standard.

Anyway, it's a rather large cost for the supplier. My supplier wasn't willing to apply for the standard and audit and pay for it all himself. On the other hand, my customer wouldn't pay it either. So I was stuck because I knew this was the only factory that produced this kind of item.

So, after a lengthy talk with the supplier I finally convinced him to do it. How did I do that?

Well, for one he always asked me for more orders and customers because he had lost business elsewhere. So I told him that if he invested in this Social Standard it would open up doors for him to many new and big customers. (Note that BSCI is currently a minimum standard for big retailers in Europe.)

He can now work with a lot more customers in Europe than he previously could. I am also happy to recommend his factory to my other European customers.

You will want your supplier to grow with you and not look for one-time deals.

There are exceptions, of course. Some suppliers are completely ignorant to suggestions and improvements that will cost them (not you) money and they are only after the quick and easy orders that make them money.

Well, if you have simple orders and plan never to order again from a certain factory then forget this strategy. But, if you want to grow your business and try to keep long lasting business relationships, it will pay off.

CHAPTER 4
COMMON MISTAKES WHEN IMPORTING

- Wrong specifications and instructions to the supplier that are not clear
- Not monitoring your orders properly (remember Chapter 30 in the Import Bible)
- Not being aware of licenses you might have to pay for (e.g., Bluetooth, Sisvel, etc.). The supplier DOES NOT INCLUDE these costs.
- Not keeping an eye on your supplier (blindly trusting him completely, meaning that he promises something in an email/phone call and you sit back and relax).
- Not having agreements about what will happen when there is a delay in shipment
- Choosing the wrong product

Clear instructions

I often kicked myself for not being thorough enough on orders in the past. At the beginning of my career I made a lot of mistakes or didn't follow through with processes and then they often backfired.

Make sure that you state your specifications and requirements to the supplier in emails and orders. Ask him to confirm if he understood exactly what you need.

Monitoring your orders

You need to monitor your order properly from YOUR side. Follow the steps provided in the "Import-Bible" and live by them. Use checklists, reminders and notebooks to monitor your orders. Make sure you have collected all information, documents, etc., for your own administration.

Licenses & certification costs

When you order a specific product group it may be that you have to pay licenses or certificates to a certain organization. For example, a Bluetooth or MP3/4 speaker needs to have a Bluetooth license and a Sisvel license. This should be paid for by the customer (you).

In most cases the supplier will not include these costs into the product and will probably not remind you about them either.

You can check with your inspection company what requirements and certifications your products need to comply with the law. If you are already working with an inspection company, then they usually provide this information for free.

In any case, make sure you check this or your products might be held up at customs or you can get a claim from the license holder.

Keep an eye on your supplier. He might promise something in an email or phone call and then forget about it. Say you are waiting for samples, an invoice or whatever you might need from him. Remind him after a few days if you haven't received any feedback.

Not having agreements when there is a delay in shipment

Many first timers forget that there could be a delay on an order and that might bring trouble. Perhaps you have a planned promotion or you promised a specific delivery day to your client.

How do you avoid or fix problems caused by a delay?

HAVE A PURCHASE ORDER TERM or separate buying agreement.

This might come in handy if you have a delay and you need to air-ship your goods to meet your deadlines (more on that in Chapter 7 on shipping).

Make sure your supplier sign this agreement or you can't claim any penalty!!

Choosing the wrong product – example of a product launch fail

Recently I heard about a colleague launching a new product.

He was looking into portable speakers. He wanted to compete with the big brands but at a price level far below the competition.

So we worked out a way for a model that has enormous sound quality but still at a price level far below the big brands. Eventually, the supplier develop the item so he could market it. He started sending out sales pitches to customers but no one was interested. He didn't understand – He thought they would be buying those things off his hands in no time.

He realized people didn't really understand the product. So he started thinking in other ways. If retailers didn't want to buy large quantities, then what about crowd funding? He looked at Kickstarter and Indiegogo. Indiegogo would be his only option as he was not based in the US and only they allow countries outside the US to make campaigns on their website.

So he went with Indiegogo. After 2 ½ months work, he was ready to launch the project.

He was so excited to post the campaign that he didn't do a lot of research to see if he had a "product-to-market-fit" prior to publishing it. He only did a lot of research on how to RUN a campaign successfully. There would be press releases, massive social traffic to be created and so forth. So for 2 weeks into the campaign working 14 hours a day on it he eventually gave up. At the end of the campaign he only reached 6% of the total funding and he refunded everyone who bought one.

What went wrong?

First, he was so enthusiastic about the idea and project he only learned later that there isn't only one but at least 5 other big brands doing this product right now. He was still competitive in pricing compared to them but he didn't really have a well-known brand behind his product.

And only 1 week before launching he saw German retailers with their own private label on very similar speakers imported from China. Even worse, they were only 49USD above his price and obviously had a bigger marketing budget than he did.

Second, he realised people want branded items if they choose such a product. The price tag in this product category didn't matter, it seemed. He did some research during the campaign and people really didn't mind paying a bit more for this kind of product. He also saw a similar project that launched a month before his. Even they didn't do that well.

Third, he had a huge problem with shipping rates. He planned on sending the produced lot to a fulfillment center in Shenzhen and they would then send the item to each customer worldwide. He also only realized at a very late stage that his first calculations on shipping rates were completely wrong! It would cost him at least 50-60 USD per piece to ship to most countries because the item was rather heavy and large (He wanted a courier with tracking service to make sure the item really got to the customer).

This caused a huge hole in his profit.

And lastly, again a research issue that he hadn't thought of in the beginning was the problem that his item wouldn't be compatible in many countries. He needed to change the plug and add an adapter so that people could use it everywhere. That was another 10USD he had to add to his price.

He ended up with a profit of 1.5USD per item (from an initial 39USD, after deducting PayPal, Indiegogo and credit card fees). And he wasn't even sure about some freight rates and problems that may occur during customs. It was an absolute nightmare.

He told me afterwards that he was happy the project didn't get more media attention; otherwise he could have ended up with a huge loss BUT he was happy he did the project because he learned a lot from it.

So what is the take away here?

- **He should have done research, research & more research**
- **He should have thought about the product-to-market fit. This obviously wasn't a product that people needed.**
- **He didn't calculate his costs accurately enough**

- He didn't pay enough attention to product requirements for each country
- He managed this whole project himself, with no outside help

I can't stress enough how important it is you do your research and validate your product idea. Make sure you calculate your costs precisely and "triple confirm" them against each supply chain step (logistics, customs, tax, fees, etc.).

And even if you have a great product and want to take it to Kickstarter or Indiegogo, DON'T do it alone. Hire someone to help you on marketing and social media publicity.

Lesson learned!

CHAPTER 5
PRICE INCREASES AND HOW TO DEAL WITH THEM

So you received an email from your supplier that prices have to be increased because the Chinese Yuan (RMB) is being appreciated, his labor costs have risen or some other reason.

Never accept any price increase blindly.

But let's first analyze the situation:

- **Has he increased the price within the last year? If yes, how often?**
- **Has he stated on his last quotation the validity of the price (see next chapter)?**
- **What are the reasons he wants to increase prices?**

Here are common reasons for price increases:

- **Labor costs need to be increased**
- **Raw material costs have increased**
- **Chinese Renminbi (YUAN) has appreciated against the USD**
- **Purchase of machinery to upgrade the factory**

Lets go through them one by one and see how you could avoid the increase or find an acceptable solution between the both of you. I also want to give you background on each so that you can understand these reasons.

135

Labor costs need to be increased:

When I moved to Hong Kong in 2005 the average salary of a worker was around 250USD per month. Yes, that's right, per month. Nowadays a worker in the production line can get up to 1000USD or sometimes more. Some of the workers earn more than the staff in the office. Factories need to pay a high salary to workers because it's so difficult to find them.

Yes, China has over 1.3 billion people but not everyone wants to stand in a workshop or production line doing rudimentary work. Education has improved a great deal since the early 2000's and people want to work in offices rather than on production lines. So factories have to reach out to far provinces to hire workers. Costs automatically rise in that process. I have been told that some factories rent a bus and drive to provinces actively hiring workers to bring them back to the factory that same day on the bus.

What can you do in that case? Honestly not much. But if a supplier keeps increasing prices because of labor costs you might want to look for another supplier who has more machinery or automated processes that require less workmanship. This can actually be more expensive (because of the investment for machinery) but you should have more stability on prices in the future.

Raw material costs have increased:

This requires a little research but if a supplier uses this reason for price increases you can quickly find out if he is lying.

Go onto websites like the following and research the price index on your product's main material:

http://www.meps.co.uk/raw%20material%20index.html

http://www.indexmundi.com/

Unfortunately, there is not much free information on the Internet; you have to pay for most services if you want real accurate data. You can also check out your local stock or commodity market online and see if you can get free data.

Once you find your product's raw material price check the development over the last few months or even years. **Compare it with the orders** that you made to your supplier at the specific price drops or increases. If for example you ordered your item before at a lower raw material price than now, you can use this information to negotiate with your supplier.

I often find that suppliers use this excuse of raw material price to increase their profit margin. When you have data that backs that the raw material price has perhaps even decreased since your last purchase, let the supplier know and share the link or information that you found. Demand the same or an even lower price than what you are paying now.

If raw material really has increased then you might want to check by how much. If the supplier's price increase does not match the actual raw material price increase, let him know and demand a lower price increase.

Chinese Renminbi (YUAN /RMB) has appreciated against the USD

The Chinese Yuan has risen over 40% since its revaluation in 2005 (when it was pegged against the USD). It has been undervalued for a long time but that has changed since the economic reforms under Deng Xiaoping. Since China opened to the rest of the world and became the world's factory the Yuan has risen a great deal.

Many factories increase prices once the Yuan gets appreciated against the USD.

If the Yuan gets appreciated against the USD it is usually in the news and you should hear about it. You can also check official USD/RMB exchange rates to verify this claim.

Not much you can do here either, except perhaps asking for one more order with the last price before you accept the new price.

Purchase of machinery to upgrade the factory

This usually doesn't happen very often, but when the factory claims there is machinery to buy to upgrade the factory it's actually a good thing for you. It will lower the labor costs over time and you should have a stable price for a while.

Ask your supplier to explain the type of machinery he is buying and how you can benefit from it in the future. Let him give you a guarantee or confirmation that this will benefit your price in the future.

CHAPTER 6
ADVANCED NEGOTIATION

Validity of prices

Always ask your supplier to give you a validity of the quoted price.

A common time frame should be 90 days, sometimes more sometimes less.

In any case, ask your supplier for a validity of 180 days (6 months). It might take you a long time to decide to order this product for various reasons.

If you get back to the supplier after a while and you haven't confirmed validity he might increase the price. That can put you in a difficult spot if you gave the quoted price to your customer. You might have to re-offer to your customer and that's never good.

Big retailers usually have 1 year or even longer terms with suppliers. They can do that because the suppliers know that the quantities will be large and retailers often take a long time to decide because of their decision chain/process.

How to avoid or battle a price increase:

Short term:

- Insist on the last order price for this order. Tell him you are about to give him a re-order.
- Look into raw material price sheets. There are free sources on the Internet. You don't even need to be updated all the time,

139

but simply look at a price curve of the main material of your product for the last few months. Has the price dropped or risen significantly? Did the supplier claim that the "xxxy" material has sharply risen? Check it out before you trust him.

Long term:

- Put measurements in place such as contracts or buying terms to which the supplier has to agree before you do business. Set up your own buying terms with, for example, a minimum validity of prices in all offers.
- Ask for bonus payments or agreements. If you know that you will be re-ordering from this factory, make a written agreement that you will receive a discount of a certain percentage from the next order based on your previous year.

Bonus payments:

It is getting more common to agree on bonus payments these days. It works the same way as back home with your local supplier. You agree on certain delivery terms, merchandising payment, back-payments and bonuses if a certain turnover is reached per year.

This usually only works with suppliers that you already work with. But you can certainly try it on any supplier. Even if you get a few hundred USD discount or bonus payment it's definitely worth it!

You could set the following simple bonus payments with your supplier:

Turnover Goal 2015: xxxxx USD
If reached, bonus payment of 5% (for example) to be discounted from the next order.

For every xxxxUSD above this amount a further 1% (for example) to a maximum of X% applies.

Send this agreement to your supplier. You can obviously work out a more detailed agreement but this is a simple illustration on how it could look.

In any case I am sure there is some bonus or discount that can be arranged on future orders. The best option would be a direct bank transfer of the bonus at the year's end but most suppliers will only agree on a discount deducted from any future order.

Other ways:

How to negotiate a good price with a low order quantity:

It is quite common that the supplier will send you a price based on a certain order quantity. Say 10USD for a quantity of 1,000 pieces. Sometimes suppliers will give you 2-3 different prices for different quantities.

If you are planning to order an item, you should have a general idea of how to negotiate when you ask your supplier for a quote. DOUBLE (2,000) or even TRIPLE (3,000) this expected order quantity when asking for a price. It's a tactic I use to see what the price range can be. If I actually order this item later at the quoted price but I am below the requested MOQ of the supplier I will pledge with the supplier to keep the price so that we can get started.

I will also mention that it will be a trial order and if everything goes well I will order the initial MOQ that the price was based on.

Perhaps the supplier will not give you the price based on your 1,000 pieces but he will give you the price based on 2,000 pieces to show his support.

This works in most cases. A supplier always will want to support you because they need to feed their factories with orders, even if they t make less profit, just to keep production running and to be cost effective.

Ask for a mixed calculation:

Say you buy 4 items from the same supplier and there is one item out of your assortment that is really price sensitive but the other 3 items are not.

Ask your supplier to keep the price on the price sensitive item the same (or decreased) and allow him to increase the other items at the same time (up to the maximum of the original price increase).

This way you can still offer the price sensitive item at the same price to your customers and lose only a little bit of profit on your higher margin items.

Advanced raw material purchase:

Many suppliers like to increase the price on your re-order.

Let him know that you have an order coming up and that he should purchase raw material now at the lowest prices and that you want to have a better price than the previous order. He may want a written order confirmation for that so that he can purchase raw material on your behalf.

Other suppliers offer on hand (or not)

If you have other suppliers' offers on hand that are cheaper than the same item from your current supplier then tell your supplier and demand at least the same price. If you don't have another offer on hand you could also pretend that you have an offer that is (say 10%) cheaper. Some suppliers may ask who it is from or if they can see it, but you don't necessarily have to send it to him.

If you do have an offer from another supplier I would actually send it to my current supplier and ask him to lower the price.

How I got 7 suppliers to pay my buyer 100,000USD in bonus payments

I had a buyer for Christmas items flying in from Austria pre-order season.

We arranged to meet up with 9 suppliers over 2 days in our office in Hong Kong. I asked the suppliers to come in and meet with us to discuss the up-coming orders and next season items. The suppliers were happy to come and meet us because we usually would place orders in excess of 100,000USD to each of them per year.

We started off each meeting the same way. We told them we would be selecting new items and then we would tell the supplier how happy we were with the previous season and that we wanted to enlarge business this year. This got them in a happy mood. We selected a few new items to add to the assortment with each supplier.

Eventually my buyer sat back and I started to talk about newly introduced bonus payments to each supplier. We wanted 10% of the last year's order amount in bonus payments to be deducted from the next order. I also prepared an agreement to fix the payments right there and then with the supplier's signature.

We sat a long time with each supplier explaining the difficult economic situation, the EUR/USD exchange rate and how this all made it difficult for the buyer to succeed in his business. We needed the supplier's support, there and then or else there might not be any increased orders. (You can always use other reasons, such as economic situations in your country, etc.)

Two suppliers wouldn't pay anything but we ended the 2 days with over 100,000USD in bonus payments (some suppliers had orders of over 300,000USD from us). This was a lot more than we expected. How did I do that?

Initially the suppliers were reluctant. Since I wasn't the actual buyer but the product manager it sure was a good thing the buyer was there. This way the supplier saw the buyer and had no way of wriggling himself out easily.

Chinese do not want to lose face in front of their customers. They often promise the "best prices / best services," etc., and it was time to prove they meant what they said. If you continually insist on a bonus and financial support they will eventually give in, because they want your future business and they don't want to upset you.

In your case, since you will be the buyer, **you see the importance of coming to China to negotiate your deals**. A negotiation like this is highly unlikely to succeed via a phone call or an email.

You don't need to have an office here. You can hold meetings and negotiations in your hotel or at the factory.

Even if your quantities or order value are not as big as the example above you still have an edge. Even the smallest discounts on your next orders could cover the airfare ticket you bought to get to China. Not to mention the suppliers you met on other days to source for new ideas. It will definitely be worth it.

Before you go into a negotiation with a supplier, plan ahead with a clear strategy similar to the one described above.

CHAPTER 7
SHIPPING & COURIER SERVICES

When does it make sense to ship what in which way?

The 3 most common shipments are done via **SEA, AIR & SEA/AIR**

Sea shipment

Sea shipment is done for most of the import/export business these days.

It is simply the most economic way to ship goods. But it is also the slowest way to ship goods.

There are generally 4 different types of container shipments. Depending on the volume of your goods you can choose from the different capacities. These are (Wikipedia Excerpt):

		20' container		40' container		40' high-cube container		45' high-cube container	
		imperial	metric	imperial	metric	imperial	metric	imperial	metric
external dimensions	length	19' 10 ½"	6.058 m	40' 0"	12.192 m	40' 0"	12.192 m	45' 0"	13.716 m
	width	8' 0"	2.438 m	8' 0"	2.438 m	8' 0"	2.438 m	8' 0"	2.438 m
	height	8' 6"	2.591 m	8' 6"	2.591 m	9' 6"	2.896 m	9' 6"	2.896 m
interior dimensions	length	18' 8 ¹³/₁₆"	5.710 m	39' 5 ⁴⁵/₆₄"	12.032 m	39' 4"	12.000 m	44' 4"	13.556 m
	width	7' 8 ¹⁹/₃₂"	2.352 m	7' 8 ¹⁹/₃₂"	2.352 m	7' 7"	2.311 m	7' 8 ¹⁹/₃₂"	2.352 m
	height	7' 9 ⁵⁷/₆₄"	2.385 m	7' 9 ⁵⁷/₆₄"	2.385 m	8' 9"	2.650 m	8' 9 ¹⁵/₁₆"	2.698 m
door aperture	width	7' 8 ⅛"	2.343 m	7' 8 ⅛"	2.343 m	7' 6"	2.280 m	7' 8 ⅛"	2.343 m
	height	7' 5 ¾"	2.280 m	7' 5 ¾"	2.280 m	8' 5"	2.560 m	8' 5 ⁴⁹/₆₄"	2.585 m
internal volume		1,169 ft³	33.1 m³	2,385 ft³	67.5 m³	2,660 ft³	75.3 m³	3,040 ft³	86.1 m³
maximum gross weight		66,139 lb	30,400 kg	66,139 lb	30,400 kg	68,008 lb	30,848 kg	66,139 lb	30,400 kg
empty weight		4,850 lb	2,200 kg	8,380 lb	3,800 kg	8,598 lb	3,900 kg	10,580 lb	4,800 kg
net load		61,289 lb	28,200 kg	57,759 lb	26,600 kg	58,598 lb	26,580 kg	55,559 lb	25,600 kg

Normally a 20' container will fit your goods in volume. But if you have larger shipments you may have to combine different container sizes.

So what suppliers do in that case is to give you the calculated volume of goods, which you will then provide to your logistics company. They will give you the best and normally the cheapest way to ship your goods.

Sometimes it makes sense to order a full container and pay a little more even though you don't have enough volume. This is because the container will only hold your goods and not anyone else's, as in LCL (low container loading). See the *Import Bible* for details.

Lets take a look at 2 examples and what to choose from in which case:

1) Your goods have a volume of 29 cubic meters.

If you take a full 20' container you would have to have 33.1 cubic meters.

But not necessarily. You can still order the full 20' container and pay a little more so that the whole container is yours.

Which means there will be no foreign goods from other customers in your container, so that the container goes directly to you and does not have to be unloaded to separate the goods. This also saves time.

You could of course take a LCL shipment, meaning that you book 29 cubic meters with your logistics company and only pay for the 29 cubic meters. But the forwarder/logistics company might fill the remaining 4.1 cubic meters with other customer's goods.

2) Your goods have a volume of 72 cubic meters.

You could either go with a:

- 40' container (67.5 cubic meters) and the rest (4.5 cubic meters) by LCL

Or

- Order a 40' high cube container (75.3 cubic meters) and pay the full price but have the container only loaded with your goods.

Now Option 1 will be probably cheaper but you have the risk that other goods might delay your shipment. Option 2 will probably be around the same price and safer for you.

What if you have a small volume like 3 cubic meters?

Depending on the following 3 factors you can either decide to sea or air ship:

- Weight
- Size/volume
- Urgency

If it is not urgent, the size and weight are not very big and you don't mind shipping by sea, you will save a lot of money if you choose sea shipment.

If it's urgent there are 2 more options:

1) SEA / AIR shipment

You can go for this option if it's semi-urgent.

It is more expensive but also shaves off more than half of the time compared to sea shipment.

Three cubic meters to an American airport can typically take 30 days via sea shipment. With SEA / AIR shipment this can take up to only 14 days.

How does that work?

Logistic companies usually have slots booked for air shipments on their freight planes or even commercial planes.

For example, if you produce an electronic toy in Shenzhen, goods will typically go from Shenzhen to Korea (Seoul) via ship and then be transported onto a plane that flies to an American city.

I do not have exact figures as they fluctuate a lot but this is usually 60% more expensive than by sea.

This option could be necessary if your supplier has delayed your shipment and you need to have the goods for a planned promotion.

If it's the supplier's fault, negotiate with him so that he takes care of the extra charges that occurred due to the delay.

> INSIDER TIP: Remember to have an agreement on your order that states there will be a penalty if there is a delay. So he either pays the penalty or makes sure that the goods arrive on time, meaning he pays for any air or air/sea shipment extra costs. Also see this part under Chapter 4 (not having agreements when there is a delay in shipment).

AIR SHIPMENT:

Now, if you have a low volume like 3 cubic meters and the goods are not too heavy then it makes sense to air-ship.

Courier services like DHL/FedEx/TNT, etc., can usually handle the entire process for you from picking up the goods, loading them onto a plane, taking care of the entire customs process and having the goods delivered to your doorstep. This is also called **"customs brokerage"** within the courier industry.

Your supplier should have a contact and preferred rate with these courier services. If not you can contact your local courier service to get a quote.

Often the cost of shipment is **calculated by volumetric weight** (for courier and express services). This can quickly become a very expensive shipping option. If the volumetric weight is higher than the declared weight, the costs will be based on the volumetric weight, **making some shipments very expensive.**

I did a calculation for one of my products as an example. It's a large Bluetooth speaker and due to its size it will be calculated in volumetric weight (4 pieces export carton / 10KG, 0.058cbm). It would be very expensive to ship it via couriers like DHL:

It would cost me around 467USD to send this sample shipment to my customer in Germany! But then again, this was a price directly from DHL's website and it didn't include any discount. Usually when you have an account you get 5-15% off your shipments, sometimes more, all depending on your turnover with them.

Unless you are a huge retailer or corporation don't book directly with these couriers. Here is how you go ahead with DHL through your factory:

I went to www.sendfromchina.com, which is a China-based fulfillment center. Remember when I mentioned that big fulfillment centers (and even your supplier) get a much better rate with courier services like DHL/FedEx/TNT?

I used the same carton weights and measurements and the indication prices were as follows:

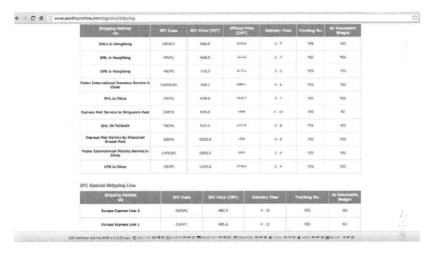

DHL was now at 109USD. And even better, when using another express line (which is most likely China Post registered air mail) the costs were even lower, at 80USD.

This example gives you an idea of how much air-shipment can cost you and what rates suppliers can get with their discounted courier prices.

Even if your suppliers don't have an account with a courier (very unlikely) you can get these rates. Simply contact your logistics provider and let him give you a quote. You can also go over to www.sendfromchina.com and check out their freight services.

Air shipment - big style

A few years ago my German customer (a very big retailer) was about to miss his planned promotion with a solar lamp because of a delay in shipment. He promoted this solar lamp on his website and advertisement flyers sent out to a few million households. The season was about to start and the goods were delayed for over a month.

Eventually the supplier had to air-ship the first lot, which was roughly a 1 x 20' container (10% of the order), because of the agreed penalty when goods are in delay. The rest was shipped out later by sea but I managed to get the urgently needed first 10% for the start of the season to be shipped by air. Once again, this points out the **need for a purchase order term** for delays or a separate **buying agreement** with penalty fees (make sure your supplier has signed this buying agreement with penalty terms).

It cost the supplier around 50,000USD to ship these 10% by air. Not something you want to do as a supplier, but he had no choice as the order was done by L/C (letter of credit) and he wouldn't get his money otherwise.

Obviously this German retailer had very large business with this supplier and was therefore able to have his way. If you are a small fish for a factory the most you could probably hope for is a percentage penalty. But you should be able to get something from the supplier.

Remember to **have buying terms and penalty agreements** on your orders with the suppliers.

CHAPTER 8
QC (QUALITY CONTROL)

What kind of quality control should you have in place?

I stressed this part already in the *Import Bible*. You **NEED** an inspection and quality control in place especially when you are placing large orders.

Why is that?

Larger retailers or buying companies usually have their sample tested professionally before placing an order. This is done either by their internal lab or a third party. If you would like to make absolutely sure that your product will conform to regulations and be up to quality standards take this step. It will usually cost you a few hundred USD, depending on the third party.

I recommend this step if your item is costly and your quantity is larger than 500 pieces or 3000USD in total value. You will usually receive a test report that you could also send to your supplier and ask for his feedback and/or improvement of the product before order placement.

Today there are many basic requirements that need to be met. For example, chemical substances in plastic or textiles that are not allowed to exceed a certain percentage within the product. Some items need to have a certain certificate (such as FCC, RoHS or CE), which means that the product is pre-approved under certain criteria and OK to import.

Of all the smaller companies that, for example, drop-ship or have smaller order quantities, I know for a fact that 95% of them don't have their items tested for chemical substances or for other technical requirements. If you drop-ship directly to your customers (for example FBA – fulfillment by Amazon) you wont get into trouble. But if you are selling to larger companies or wholesalers they will probably ask you for test reports.

If you (or the third party) found anything that you would like to change or have explained ask your supplier to look into this, either to improve the product quality or to give you feedback on any problems. To make sure that the supplier will fix any problems, indicate to him that (in case of an order) you will check this during the inspection (performed by third party; see Chapter 23).

Bear in mind if you are a start-up or planning your first import this step **may not be necessary** as it adds cost to your product.

However, if you have existing business and are trying to expand through larger importing this is an absolute must.

Depending on your product you can check general requirements here: https://importdojo.com/import-dojo-certification/

My Certifications course aims to educate you about requirements and regulations in your home country. With this course you'll be able to understand how certifications and regulations work.

Make an agreement with your supplier in the beginning of your business relationship. This should include, for example, that you will pay for the first shipment inspection and if it fails, the supplier is responsible for the re-inspection (if you wish to have one).

Many larger suppliers also have an in-house inspection teams or even laboratories. Some even have certified laboratories through third-party inspection companies. Ask your supplier what his QC procedures are and let him explain them to you.

Here is an example from Switzerland's largest retailer on how they ask for a quote from new suppliers (in this case that was me). Obviously I wouldn't recommend you to be so precise when sending your first QC requirements to your supplier. It will only confuse him, especially if it is a small factory with no or little experience with western customers. I admit this example is a bit extreme, but that's how the big retailers work with factories in China.

===============

We are now looking for a good supplier who can supply us the **BEST QUALITY products** for Switzerland market.

1-2 functional samples (full set) should be provided to xxxxx HK upon requested and they are for quality verification before placing the order.

Your offer products must be free to third parties. Supplier shall undertake to bear all costs and losses incurred in this respect.

Kindly send us the price in our offer sheet in attached, together with the product spec for our reference.

Please quote on FOB port basis, TT / LC AT SIGHT payment on a quantity as above, included 2% of Free of Charge units and mention that what kind of sales packaging and also include export carton costs into your price, which also included the **C/O-FTA**, all valid testing certificates + reports and all the related license fee if applicable. Offers shall be valid at least 3 months.

Products will be printed with our OEM logo.
Standard guarantee for the products by suppliers is 2 years.

Sales packaging is included gift box and user manual in 3 different languages – 4C printing.

The round transparent of "Original" label shall be enclosed the opening of gift box/blister.

The quality of export carton must be strong enough, min double-ply thick in order to pass the drop test. 2 of TU labels printed with project info shall be adhered in outers.

Max gross weight per export carton is 25kg. Export carton size shall be matched to the half Euro pallet in 60 x 40cm max. Products that jut out on the pallets are not tolerated.

Never use PVC for packaging what also INCLUDED tapes and stickers

European testing regulation needs to be fulfilled by your products including the packaging, and suppliers should provide their existing test reports for any update standard(s) that is/are required by law "legal & market requirements". ErP and **RoHS** as a part of legal regulation, related test reports shall be provided. REACH and RoHS must be complied. Besides, *PAH, Phthalates and Organotin test reports shall be provided for reference purpose if any.*

Inspection and random checks from different products out of inline and or final inspections will be carried to insure the products can comply the law requirements under AQL standard. Drop test will be applied at least 3 export cartons.

Inline 20% and FRI 100% of well packed products in export cartons (Ready to ship) per shipment by xxxxx QC.

Costs of Re-inspection, due to rejections, will be at supplier's cost.

The Inspection Certificate (IC) will be issued by xxxxx HK QC team after the positive FRI result is done.

Any questions related to the inspection issue, please feel free to contact our xxxxx HK QC team at

Supplier shall undertake the Product Liability Insurance. An insured sum of not less than CHF 5 million per personal/material injury or loss (combined loss), whereby the insured sum shall not limit the third-party liability of the supplier.

Supplier/factory is obliged to comply with the Code of Conduct of the BSCI www.bsci-intl.org , and to permit the appropriate controls.
If supplier/factory has the BSCI report, please send it to us as reference. We will visit the factory to assure that the product is produced under the xxxxx requirements, in all sub-factories as well.

Kuehne + Nagel Ltd. is our nominated forwarder for the shipments arrangement.

- Preproduction sample in final full packing – at least 2 pcs of each color and per model (before production)
- Production Sample - at least 2 pcs of each color and per model (before inspection)
- Shipment Sample - at least 1 pc of each color and per model (during the inspection)

You can take out a few examples of this email and apply them to your supplier. I recommend especially the part where they tell the supplier that if you fail the inspection, the costs are on them. "*Costs of Re-inspection, due to rejections, will be at supplier's cost*"

I can tell you for a fact that 70% of the suppliers who receive this inquiry will not reply. Not because they don't want the business but because they will not be able to comply with the standards and requirements of the big retailers. If they do reply they most likely haven't read through half of the email and are simply ignoring the requirements for now, hoping they could do business anyway. But this retailer will eliminate suppliers at a certain stage that can't comply to their standards 100%.

CHAPTER 9
PROPER ALIBABA SUPPLIER IDENTIFICATION

In addition to the *Import Bible* Part 1chapter on Alibaba and Global Sources, here are a few more tips.

I often get asked how do you determine if a supplier is legitimate or not? How do I know if he will he scam me or if he is a real manufacturer? There are many ways to develop a gut feeling and there are a few ways to make absolutely sure that you won't get scammed.

Alibaba is the largest supplier database in the world. Naturally a lot of middleman/scammers are on there as well.

They hide among millions of supplier listings and it is difficult to filter out the right ones. I covered the basics already in the *Import Bible* Part 1.

Here are some steps that help you filter out these middlemen and scammers:

Look at the company profile. There is a lot of information that you can take away from that page. Also, there is a lot of information that might lead you to immediately establish if something is off or fishy.

Check if there is a **Management Standard** (such as ISO9001 or BSCI). If there is no standard mentioned you might as well skip this supplier (or middleman) altogether. If there is a standard, ask for the certification. Pay attention to the name issued on the certification. A middleman/scammer will not invest in such a standard.

Look at the supplier's **product categories**. Does he specialize in a few product categories or does he have hundreds of different products, from bananas to computers? It's usually a sign that it is a trading company if they have a lot of different products.

What about **registered capital?** Some suppliers will mention their registered capital. If a supplier has a registered capital of say 50,000RMB but he has an annual turnover of 50Mil. USD something doesn't add up.

Remember also that some suppliers are pre-verified by Alibaba or another third party (even on-sight at the factory). This should help you when selecting as well.

I am not saying that all the information on the Alibaba **company profiles is accurate**. If Alibaba verifies it, this is only sometimes done through an email or a phone call. Email the supplier and ask him to send you his latest audit or report done from a third party.

I think you will get a feeling right from the start for who might be a middleman or scammer. If numbers, pictures, or anything else doesn't add up, beware.

If I get the feeling communication is difficult or if he only follows up my **questions with answers in fragments** that are usually the biggest no nos for me. The factory standard is usually a certificate available also in English that is easy to verify yourself. Compare addresses and names on the certificate with the address you have. If it doesn't add up... you know it.

The business license is usually in Chinese so it is a bit more difficult to verify. If he is refusing to send it, it's a sign he is just a trader (or scammer) and doesn't want you to know it.

Make them **produce a customized sample** for you that they do not have on hand and have them video Skype with you. Simple things can go a long way towards legitimizing who you are dealing with.

Lets take a look at an example with a supplier that I would feel comfortable working with.

This supplier has been established for 12 years. I don't really care if he is a Gold Supplier for only 1 year, it doesn't mean anything.

What interest me are the verifications from third parties and his main customers.

Quick facts:

- The annual turnover makes sense for a 12-year-old company.
- Their main markets fit with my customers.
- They have the necessary factory standards that I need for my customers (ISO 9001& 14001).

- Their main customers are big name customers (Wal-Mart, Best Buy), which puts me at ease because I know they have very high requirements.

- They have third-party supplier assessments and reports from TUV-Rhineland, which is one of the leading third party inspection companies from Germany.

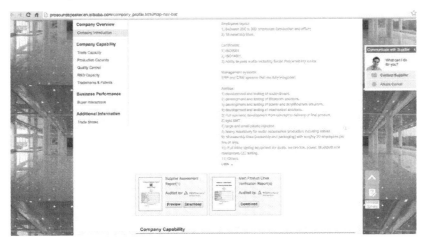

- I check and the report is valid.

Also, if I am serious about a supplier, I will give him a call. During the call I ask many questions, such as who do they work with, their annual production capacity, their certifications, etc.

I will then **develop a "gut" feeling** before I move on.

I often come across supplier profiles that don't make sense. Either their turnover is huge (compared to their 15 workers) or other data doesn't add up.

You will **develop a "gut" feeling** after a while on Alibaba.

> **TIP:** If you are unsure of the supplier's honesty and not sure about prices or if he is legitimate, make them produce a customized sample for you that they do not have on hand and have them video Skype with you.

The next logical step before placing an order would be to visit the factory.

Since that might not be possible for you, you should consider booking a factory audit with a third party inspection company (depending on the turnover or order amount).

Trading companies on Alibaba:

Working with a trading company on Alibaba

Don't eliminate a supplier because he has "trading" somewhere in his name. It is quite common that many factories do not have an export license, which is necessary if they want to sell overseas.

In this case they will hire a "trading company" that deals with their export affairs. The "trading company" will charge the factory a small percentage in order to issue documents such as licenses and trade on behalf of the manufacturer with you.

There is one way you can tell trading companies from real manufacturers. Trading companies put the name of their hometown within their company registration. Manufacturers, on the other hand, use the province name. For example: "Ningbo Better Lighting Company" (made up name) is probably a trading company but "**Zhejiang** Ningbo Better Lighting Company" is probably a manufacturer.

CHAPTER 10
LEGAL REQUIREMENTS & CERTIFICATIONS ON PRODUCTS

The basic information on legal requirements and certifications is covered in the *Import Bible*.

I will give a few more examples here:

In the early 1990's when import from China really started to boom it was very easy to import goods. I didn't experience it myself but my first boss in Hong Kong told me when they started their company in 1991, buyers wouldn't ask for any certifications, samples or testing reports. They simply sent an Excel file with a price and a picture and got an order. Sometimes they would also get orders right on the spot when they exhibited or when customers came to their showroom.

A lot has certainly changed since then. Governments these days regulate nearly every product. Products need to fulfill strict laws, regulations and certification statuses. Europe is a pioneer in enforcing new laws and regulations, especially related to electrical products.

This comes from the European Directive of Energy related products (ErP). It prohibits items from having a certain level of energy consumption. The ultimate goals of this directive are the reduction of energy consumption and making products more economical.

It can be a headache for suppliers as many of these regulations are "made up" somewhere in Brussels by a "team of specialists" that have no relation to the manufacturing industry in China.

Many regulations are difficult to apply to products and sometimes they even mean that a factory will go out of business.

There is no question that these lawmakers have a common goal. Namely, to protect the environment and their citizens. It is certainly not easy for Chinese suppliers to keep up with the regulations and ongoing new requirements.

A good example is the regular incandescent bulb. They have already been phased out in most of Europe and the US since 2011. LED bulbs are the new light source for the coming years. But even these LEDs have requirements that get more and more strict over time. Suppliers that are established will oblige and keep up with requirements but small factories will struggle.

It is essential that you have a supplier that keeps up with requirements and standards. If he doesn't know what they are but you want him to apply them, you can get him in touch with third party inspection/laboratory companies like TUV, SGS, BUREAU VERITAS, ASIA INSPECTION and so on.

If you are about to select a new supplier make sure that he knows what you need and what the requirements in your countries are. If he doesn't, explain it to him, that is, if you want to work with him.

Before I start sourcing for a new product I usually check the **minimum requirements with my contact at a third party inspection company.**

I then send my requirements and product ideas to the supplier and ask in the first email if he can comply with them. If he cannot and has no idea about these requirements I usually eliminate him in the first sourcing round. If I have no choice and have to take this supplier (because he might be the only one supplying the type of product) I will try to educate him and help him to understand the requirements.

Important: Make sure that you get a reply/confirmation to your quality requirements in your emails. Often when I send out a new sourcing request to a supplier I get an email back with an Excel sheet that includes a price and some specifications. The answers to my product requirements can often not be found anywhere.

Email or call him back and ask him about the quality or legal requirements that you sent. I usually call in that situation via Skype and have a quick talk.

If he simply forgot or didn't read it in the first email AND he confirms he can comply ask him to send you test reports or certificates.

Check these and if you are unsure on how to read them or if you don't understand them, send them to your third-party inspection company for checking.

I had 2 cases in the past where a supplier sent me certificates and only too late did I find out that these **were forged**. This can be checked **through your third party inspection company**. I use my contact at the third party inspection company for a quick check, and it usually costs me nothing.

If you are importing in small quantities you still have to fulfill certain requirements if you are in a B2B industry, whether it is for textiles, furniture, ceramics or others. Some product categories (such as electronics) can be very strict and complicated. If you sell online B2C such as Amazon or EBay you technically still need to meet them, as you are the importer of the goods. But, it is unlikely that your end customer (e.g,. your buyer on EBay) will send the product they bought for testing.

In most cases the suppliers have basic certificates and test reports that allow you to import goods into your country. This could be a CE, FCC or RoHS certificate, among others.

CHAPTER 11
ANTI-DUMPING RATES

To protect the local industry some products have a very high tax rate on import. These are called "anti-dumping" rates. Dumping in this case refers to overseas suppliers flooding/dumping products into the local market with prices that are far below the local suppliers.

Local suppliers complained to government agencies and they enacted "anti-dumping rates."

These rates have been in effect for a while now (since 1994) and apply to quite a few products. Essentially, it means that products bought from overseas (especially China) become even more expensive (after import tax) than prices of the local supplier. It really differs from country to country but here are a few examples of items that have a high anti-dumping rate in many countries:

- **Batteries**
- **Solar lamps or solar cell components**
- **Steel**

You can also check on www.simplyduty.com or on your local customs tariff government section. See how under the *Import Bible* Part 1 section "Calculate your costs."

Avoid products with a high tax rate or anti-dumping rate. It is likely that you have a major competitor in your country or that the tax rate will kill your profits.

CHAPTER 12
PRODUCT LIABILITY INSURANCE

Once you start importing larger quantities and perhaps on a private label you may want to consider product liability insurance.

Some suppliers have product liability insurance or are asked by their customers to apply for it (as in my earlier example with the Swiss retailer).

Product liability insurance (http://en.wikipedia.org/wiki/Product_liability) covers the loss incurred due to a problem with your products.

If you are importing large quantities regularly I also recommend you look into this with your trusted insurance company. There are a few within China/Hong Kong that provide this service if you don't find anything locally.

So what does that mean and what does it cover?

Say you are importing a product from China to the United States, to sell this product to another business, importer, retailer or online shop and suddenly one day you have a serious problem – a customer or business suing you for your sold product.

This could be because of a defect in the product that caused bodily harm, destruction of property or other serious issues. The terms are defined in the Wiki link above.

Not only because of the moral issue of bodily harm but also the financial impact, this could become a serious problem.

The first step is obviously to figure out what caused the problem. Is it a singular incident? What part of the product caused the problem?

Check if this particular problem was found during the inspection. If yes, why wasn't it reworked or why was it accepted? If no, why weren't you made aware of the problem? You could successfully blame your third party inspection company if you have a strong case of negligence.

If you didn't have an inspection or were not aware of the problem your product liability insurance comes in handy. Usually you can take out this insurance for just a group or for all of your products. Some can cover up to 5Million USD. It really depends on your insurance policy.

Normally your insurance would come into effect now to cover these losses or lawsuits.

CHAPTER 13
PRODUCTS THAT DO NOT
MAKE SENSE TO IMPORT

Some items really **don't make sense** to import (together with the anti-dumping rate items).

These items are usually license-required items, large items or items that are manufactured in a low-income country near you. China is getting some competition from a few countries, not only because of labor costs but also due to government import restrictions (mentioned under the section on anti-dumping).

Products that are difficult for importing:

- **Anything related to gas**
- **Cars**
- **Supplements**
- **Foods, drinks**
- **Animals**
- **Guns, weaponry**
- **Hazardous material**
- **And more**

For the above items you would need to obtain proper licenses first and this can be quite difficult.

Here are a few examples on emerging markets you can also import from if your product is of a large nature with high logistic costs from China:

Mexico:

Did you know that there is massive production in a few parts of Mexico of household appliances and other consumer electronics?

That's right, a large portion of appliances for the American household comes from Mexico these days. Many big names such as Electrolux, Miele, and Bosch have set up tents (factories) and are producing at large capacity.

The proximity to the US makes it an ideal purchasing market for American companies. Even though the labor costs are higher, the logistic costs are a lot lower than goods from China, making it ideal for small importers.

Large household appliances especially make sense to produce in Mexico.

For example, washing machines and refrigerators. The logistic costs on importing these items from China are immensely high compared to Mexico.

Large quantities still make sense to import from China, as the amount of pieces will drive the logistic costs down.

Turkey & Eastern Europe:

Turkey also has a large production industry but it is not limited to household appliances. Many other categories are produced in Turkey (textiles, ceramic, bathroom items). Even the big names like H&M, Zara, etc., produce in Turkey.

Turkey has a very strict policy on imports. Their import procedures including necessary documents and tax rates makes it a nightmare to import from Turkey. This way they protect the local industry, which in turn definitely benefits citizens of Turkey.

Quite a few Western European retailers buy a lot of goods from Turkey these days.

Eastern Europe also has some production facilities and due to their low labor costs it is quite affordable for importers within Western Europe to buy from there.

CHAPTER 14
MAKING PROTOTYPES / MOCK UP SAMPLES

I covered OEM/ODM already in the *Import Bible*. If you read that, you should understand the difference between OEM (closed) and ODM (open) products.

If you have a design idea it doesn't necessarily mean you immediately need to invest in toolings just to make samples. Having said that, you can't simply give a design to a factory and assume they will make you a prototype or a sample in a few days.

A lot of factories can hand **make samples these days** in their workshop.

Some more advanced factories even have rapid prototype machines.

Prototype machines obviously make non-working samples, but it could be enough to take photos for marketing or sales purposes.

Handmade samples can be made to work but the product may not be as nice **as one that has been mass manufactured.** But, with a handmade sample, you can get a pretty good idea on the final outlook and can decide based on that if you want to go ahead with mass production or not.

If your supplier does not have the means to create a prototype or sample you can go to: http://www.star-prototype.com/

This company has a huge range of services available and you can request a quote with them based on your requirements. Simply contact them and state your details.

CHAPTER 15
PRIVATE LABELS, BRANDS & TRADING NO-NAME ITEMS

There are 3 different business models that could work for you:

1) No Name, 2) Private label and 3) Brands

What's a brand?

A brand would be, for example: Samsung, Bosch, Apple, Toyota, Philips and so on.

A brand is usually a company and can be well recognized in the media.

Private label

What's a private label? Private label means that a company has created a separate label of their brand and the manufacturer/supplier is printing the private label name on a gift box or even has a label with the name of your brand on the product.

An example of a private label is the US based company and brand "**Monster Inc.**" with its private label "**BEATS** by Dr. Dre"; Monster is the original company / brand with the product and manufacturing knowledge and they teamed up with Dr. Dre to create **BEATS**.

Technically you can select a product off the rack from a supplier and ask him to make a custom gift box with your brand or private label on it. But it is likely that if you can buy it off the shelf from the supplier, that others can do so too. Perhaps you will want to work on an exclusivity contract for your country.

Also be aware that a gift box print with a private label usually requires a minimum of 1,000 pieces.

It's **not the requirement of the factory** but the requirement of the printing company. Most printing companies in China will not print color boxes below 800 pieces. It simply gets very expensive if your quantity is below that.

How I started my own private label

When I created **Mandarin-Gear** I had a vision of creating a brand that will be recognized as affordable and high quality. But I was also in need of more customers and wanted to make them trust in "Chinese quality products." I needed a product and a brand that customers could trust in terms of quality, service and follow up.

The idea was to **be inexpensive but still offer high quality products**.

When I decided on consumer electronics I looked at the manufacturers and what they offered. There were a few that had quality products but lacked the marketing and sales experience to become bigger or attract more customers. They were sitting back and waiting for customers to come.

They also created products that didn't fit the market. Apart from the standard items that sold well, they had a few innovative products but the finishing and quality was often poor or not attractive for big buyers.

So I started to talk to 1 of my suppliers about my idea and what I wanted to do. I didn't want him to OEM or design something for me.

I took **his existing product** to make it better and sell it myself. So the next step was to think how to achieve that.

I didn't have enough money to invest in designs, new tooling and heavy marketing. BUT, I could take the supplier's product and make it more attractive for buyers.

Here is what I did on my first project with a Bluetooth speaker:

- **I changed the color of the product to a more appealing one**
- **I asked him for the up-cost in a better driver & speaker to have better sound**
- **I asked my friend to create a layout/packaging for me based on my ideas. I knew nice packaging is half the work of getting sales.**
- **I prepared presentations and a few PDFs with nice photos and detailed descriptions**
- **I revised the instruction manual with proper content and grammar**

When I thought about the packaging, I knew I wanted something that really stands out and that people would love. So one day when I was out grocery shopping I grabbed a product off a shelf and saw the nutrition facts on the back of the product. This was something that could work!

I gave the idea to my design company and asked him to put the "nutrition facts" of my product on the packaging. I put the essential technical information on it and came up with a few fun facts too.

Here is an example of what my packaging looks like:

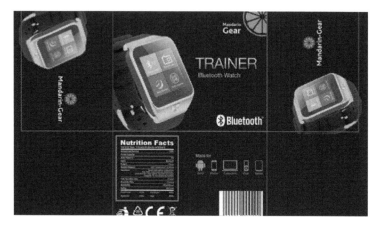

All of this didn't cost me anything and I had a very presentable product already. I took this method and used it on about 15 products, which made up my first catalogue.

It really astonishes me that Chinese suppliers have so little knowledge of western trends and how customers perceive their products. The first sample I saw of that Bluetooth speaker looked so cheap because it had shiny plastic finishing.

When it came to my finishing I was really happy with the idea to have rubber finish. It gave the product a completely new look and the impression of high quality.

Remember, this was all on paper. I didn't actually ask the supplier for a new color sample, change the finishing, improve the sound quality or print my packaging. But, I did all these steps to see if I could find customers based on my modifications.

I did ask for the costs of every process, be it the color box print, the upgrade in components in the product or the MOQ needed on my specific color. When I got the first feedback from customers I made samples.

This process applies to pretty much every product, a household appliances, fitness gear, clothing, tools or whatever. The products are ready, but there are so many options to make a much nicer product out of an existing item. Think outside the box.

Look at a product from a supplier and think about what would it take for you as a consumer to buy it. But remember to keep it realistic and not to change the entire product in the process.

This was the easy part. Now I needed to make sales.

If you are just starting with a private label you can also ask your factory to print a digital print of your private label gift-box so you can show it to your customers or check it out yourself. Digital printing is usually rather expensive and can be up to 40USD per piece.

I did some digital printing myself in the early days of my company to show customers how my brand/private label looks. Here is a look at a few gift boxes that I had digitally printed:

As you can see it's not perfect, there are a few air bubbles and wrinkles, but it does the job of showing the product in the packaging to customers.

No name packaging:

When you start off importing you are probably selling items off the rack (no-name items) from the supplier bought through Aliexpress or Alibaba.

Usually these items have the manufacturer's "brand" or even just a simple white box when they are shipped to you.

A manufacturer's brand or no-name brands are not really brands. They are simply the manufacture's name on the packaging with no or little meaning to your end-consumer. You can see a perfect example of a "Chinese brand" here:

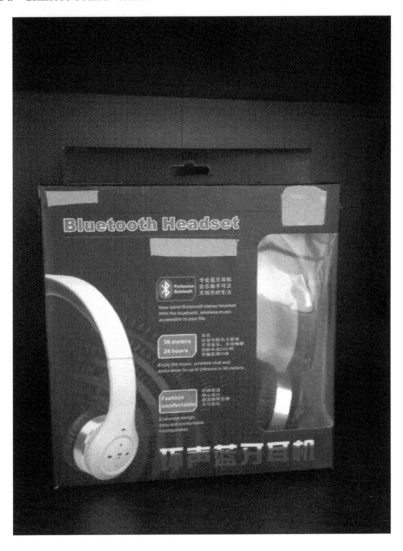

Which type of business model makes me the most money and which one should I choose?

Well if you are just starting out it probably doesn't make sense to create a brand or a private label because no one knows you yet and they have never heard of the brand/private label that you created.

Once you start selling larger quantities and have bigger customers (online and offline) you will want to **introduce a private label.**

You probably want to **start out with drop-shipping smaller quantities** through Aliexpress. If possible ask the supplier if he has a neutral packaging, perhaps a white box. If your quantities are very low, say 5-50 pieces it is very likely that you have to go with the supplier's packaging. Drop-shipping the no-name brand will make you a nice small profit on each of your products. But it's always a calculated profit, as you need to keep competitive within the market.

In most cases of no-name packaging, this is some really un-attractive packaging with horrible grammar and English on it (just like the previous example on the earlier page).

What you could ask the supplier is to have stickers made with your company name on them to be placed over the supplier's name/brand on the box.

If you are **ready to place larger orders** to your supplier in the range of 100-500 pieces you should be able to request a neutral packaging for yourself. This could be a white box with a color sticker and your logo on it.

I would also recommend Alibaba suppliers for that and not Aliexpress as Aliexpress items are usually items in stock with a supplier's packaging. Plus you don't get to inspect your shipment from Aliexpress.

Once you have quantities in the range from 500-1000 pieces you should be thinking about a private label or a brand packaging. You will want to have a packaging that sells the products itself without you doing too much. Private labels will **make you the most profit**. People trust brand names and are willing to spend more money on high-quality product/packaging.

Take a look at the packaging above from my company. It cost me nothing to design and create (apart from the printing costs). I gave the designer the input and general idea what I wanted and he duplicated the design on each of my products.

You can also ask your factory to design packaging for you based on your ideas. Every factory has a design department but it is likely that your design will be heavily "Asian-themed," meaning that it's not really attractive.

So I recommend that you take a few hundred USD and pay a professional packaging designer to create a brand or private label. There are a lot of freelance designers on websites like: www.upwork.com or www.fiverr.com.

Obviously if you are selling online only and your customers don't really need to see your packaging before buying you don't need a private label packaging.

But if you are selling larger quantities to retailers, supermarkets or wholesalers they will more likely buy from you if you have a nice packaging.

If you do have your private label ask your factory to always print at the same printing factory. Give the factory your artwork files, pantone colors and other details (provided by your designer). The reason for doing so is that you will want your packaging to always look the same.

If your packing is printed in different printing factories it is very likely that the color or printing will differ each time.

CHAPTER 16
INSTRUCTION MANUALS (IF APPLICABLE)

Once you are ready to order a product more often and in larger quantities it makes sense to have a proper instruction manual for your customers (to be included in your gift box).

Obviously not every product needs an instruction manual but they may have tags (e.g., clothing).

I have seen a lot of instruction manuals from Chinese factories and many of them are embarrassing in terms of grammar and English.

Ask your supplier to send you the instruction manual or label and take a look at it. If it isn't too much information to be translated or checked, do it yourself. If it's a lot or you don't want to do it, send it for translation or editing services. www.fiverr.com has a lot of these services available for 5USD.

Trust me, it makes a much better impression if your customer opens the package and there are easy to understand instructions included.

You probably get more positive feedback too as a seller on Amazon or EBay for that. It's the little things that make you stand out from the crowd.

CHAPTER 17
KEEPING TRACK OF YOUR PAYMENTS / INVOICES & EXPENSES

Whenever you have an expense, invoice, payment or receipt make sure you save a digital copy on your computer. I keep a very organized structure of my expenses, invoices, etc. I do this because I might need to reference them later as well as for tax reasons.

Also I keep a separate "expenses" folder for sample payments. Most suppliers charge for a sample when you order with them and before I agree to pay for a sample I will confirm with him that he will refund the sample costs on first order. It might not seem like much at the time but when you have 30-40 sample payments a year (or more) it really adds up and makes a difference if you can get the costs refunded.

CHAPTER 18
FACTORY STANDARDS (ISO, BSCI, SA8000...)

Factories themselves also need to (or should) comply with certain standards. The government does not set these standards but they are for reputation, safety and organizational purposes.

Retailers usually pay a lot of attention to factory standards. It also helps you to identify if a factory is operating within international standards.

In my previous job my buyers actually eliminated factories based on their standards, even if that factory was the only factory for a certain product.

So what do these standards mean?

These standards help you to identify a factory's dedication to business development and social compliance. If a factory has no standards at all it is usually because they have no money to invest or don't have business overseas. Even for Chinese buyers it would be a turn-off if a factory doesn't have a minimum standard of ISO 9001.

These standards are basically a quality management system (QMS) that helps to organize a factory and its processes. There are guidelines to be met from the International Organization for Standardizations : (http://en.wikipedia.org/wiki/International_Organization_for_Standa rdization).

Factories can apply for a certification from a third party inspection company (such as TUV, Bureau VERITAS, etc.) to have their factory undergo an audit by these inspection companies. If the factory complies with the standards they will be awarded a certification valid for a certain period (1-3 years).

If they do not comply they will have to re-work the "failed" issues within the organization until they comply to receive a certification.

If a factory can achieve a high status of standard such as SA8000 it is not necessary to have a standard of ISO9001, as SA8000 covers everything below this standard and more.

Many big retailers or corporations showcase social compliance on their websites. It's all about showing the general public that **"we treat our employees fairly," "we produce in green ways" and "we are socially compliant,"** by not purchasing from factories below a certain social standard.

Standards of factories

ISO 9001

To begin with this is the absolute **MUST** standard for a factory these days.

It is actually very easy to obtain. Among others these would be the 6 main processes that they need to comply with (excerpt from Wikipedia):

- Control of Documents (4.2.3)
- Control of Records (4.2.4)
- Internal Audits (8.2.2)
- Control of Nonconforming Product / Service (8.3)

188

- Corrective Action (8.5.2)
- Preventive Action (8.5.3)

You can read more here on Wikipedia: http://en.wikipedia.org/wiki/ISO_9000.

ISO 14001

This standard is a bit more difficult to obtain and it focuses more on environmental management than quality. You can read in more detail here on Wikipedia:

http://en.wikipedia.org/wiki/ISO_14000#ISO_14001_standard

BSCI

BSCI stands for Business Social Compliance Initiative and it focuses on social compliance, meaning basic things like: do the workers have access to fresh water, is food provided, do they have strict policies on child labor, and much more.

As of today, most European retailers will only work with factories that have this standard. A factory can apply for this standard but has to meet a lot of strict criteria and it is very common that factories fail at the first or even second audit. I would guess that around 10-15% of China's factories have this standard. So, if you work with a factory with this standard you should be in good hands. Read more here: http://www.bsci-intl.org/

SA8000

SA8000 is the holy grail of standards. If a factory has this standard it is probably at a higher production management and organization level than most factories in the western world. I personally only know 5 factories in China that have this standard. Obviously this standard is very expensive to maintain.

Factories with that standard usually have a lot of incentives for employees such as training or management trainee programs, excursions, free English classes, dormitory for the workers on site, free lunch, etc. It also means that you are paying a premium price for your product.

But if you were in the right niche this would be your ideal supplier. I cannot give you a name but I have been to this one SA8000 factory twice and I have never seen anything like it in China.

They produce coffee machines for the biggest brands in the world like Nespresso, Bosch, Krupp's, Philips and much more. These brands can obviously not afford a lot of return from their customers so they need top-notch quality. This one factory has a 0.8% return on most of their products, which is insanely low. Most factories have a return of 8-15%.

If you are starting out you don't need the fancy factories but if you are importing larger quantities and building a name for yourself you should have **at least ISO9001 or even better BSCI standardized** factories to work with.

Working with a factory that has a certain high standard doesn't mean you are safe in all aspects but it gives you a better feeling when you know there is some quality, social or economic management behind your production.

After all, even if you want to buy cheap from China you wouldn't want your items to be produced by a child or have the factory dump all their waste into a nearby river.

CHAPTER 19
SUBCONTRACTORS & RAW MATERIAL SUPPLIERS

Beware of sub-suppliers/contractors and make sure that your supplier receives proper raw material.

Your factory is obviously not making the whole product them-selves. Most factories outsource their material, workmanship, tools and even assembly.

It is simply too expensive these days to manufacture and assemble everything in house. Therefore, factories will most likely buy raw materials, tools, components, etc., outside and then assemble within their factory.

It is important to know that all materials and components come from a reliable source and that your assembling factory has quality controls in place. This step should assure that all components of your product are either certified or come from a source that complies with your standards and requirements.

Ask your supplier which **in house quality control** he has in place for incoming material. A good supplier usually has quality checks at his warehouse. After all, he also doesn't want to get scammed from his raw material supplier. Ask to see the certificates of the incoming raw material.

It doesn't matter if you understand what's written on the report but it will make the supplier think twice before he scams you with cheap material.

You can actually give the report to your third party inspection company for a quick review. Or you could send it to someone you trust who speaks Chinese to check it for you.

CHAPTER 20
USING PROPER (INTERNAL) SUPPORTING DOCUMENTS

You probably noticed how much attention I pay to administration and supporting documents. That wasn't always the case but I learned through many mistakes that keeping everything organized from day one of a project makes life a lot easier.

Here is what I keep on file to have total overview of my orders, products and suppliers

Product Excel Spread Sheet (or shopping list)

I keep a list of all product ideas with a picture, link where I saw it, price and some more details. Keep track of your product ideas. Make remarks on what you think is good about it, what the margin could be and so on.

I use it for research but also for sourcing. I will go into detail later about the shopping list.

Order forms (To & from)

For each order I place or receive I keep an order follow up checklist. You can find it on https://importdojo.com/importdojo-masterclass/

General Checklist

For each sourcing project I work with my ImportDojo Checklist. You will find it on https://importdojo.com/importdojo-masterclass/

Supplier forms

I use a "vendor profile" that I send in a blank format to every supplier that I think I will do business with. He can input all necessary information like: annual production capacity, turnover, staff, product categories, customers, etc. You will find it on https://importdojo.com/importdojo-masterclass/

Offers

I use a general quotation sheet for all of my customers. It includes pictures, weight, dimensions, detailed descriptions, container details, etc. You will find it on https://importdojo.com/importdojo-masterclass/

CHAPTER 21
PRODUCTION AREAS IN CHINA

I mentioned a few examples in the *Import Bible* already and you may need this information for your next trip to China. You should know where the main production areas are and what the disadvantages are for each one.

- **Guangdong province** (South of China): Electronics of any kind, especially consumer and household, toys
- **Zhejiang province** (Shanghai area): DIY products, tools, metal and fabrics, lighting
- **Hebei province** (Beijing area): Textiles, coal, steel, iron, engineering, chemicals, power, ceramics and food

These are the main areas for production.

Let's look into each one and a few others with a bit of background on the province:

Guangdong province (South of China):
http://en.wikipedia.org/wiki/Guangdong

Guangdong province, often referred to as "Canton," has 4 main production cities: Guangzhou, Dongguan, Shenzhen and Zuhai. Each of these areas has literally thousands of suppliers. There are also over 105 million people living there, most of them working in the manufacturing or hotel industry.

It is difficult to pinpoint which factory is in which city as they are all over the place.

- Household appliances (toaster, blender, hair-dryer, fans, etc.)
- Lighting (indoor & outdoor decorative, LED, contemporary)
- Toys (plus plastics, kids toys, etc.)
- Furniture (chairs, tables, outdoor furniture)
- Consumer electronics (mobile phones and accessories, tablets, etc.)
- Bathroom items (ceramics, toilet accessories, shower cabinets, etc.)

Zhejiang province (Shanghai area):

http://en.wikipedia.org/wiki/Zhejiang#Economy

Zhejiang province has 4 main production areas in and around Shanghai, Hangzhou, Ningbo and Shaoxing.

- DIY tools (garden tools, vacuum cleaners, household tools)
- Metal and wood tools (workshop tools, wood working tools)
- Fabrics and textiles (T-shirts, jackets, jeans etc.)
- Lighting (outdoor lighting, luminaries, stainless steel products, solar)
- Tea (Hangzhou area)

Hebei province (Beijing area):

http://en.wikipedia.org/wiki/Hebei#Economy

Hebei province focuses a lot on the below categories. There are many heavy-duty product factories in and around Beijing, which results in a lot of smog and polluted air. Most of the factories that use natural resources are situated in the Hebei province.

- Raw materials and natural resources (coal, steel, iron, etc.)
- Engineering

- Chemicals
- Power
- Ceramics
- Agriculture and food
- Textiles (high quality textiles, function wear, etc.)

Fujian province (South East):
http://en.wikipedia.org/wiki/Fujian#Economy

- Tea production
- Clothing and sports accessories manufacturers
- High quality technology (Boeing, Dell, GE, Kodak, Siemens, etc.)
- Decorative items (Christmas, seasonal items)
- Furniture (outdoor/garden/indoor)

Shandong province (Middle East)
http://en.wikipedia.org/wiki/Shandong - Economy

- Cotton / textiles
- Agriculture
- Precious metals

Henan province (East)
http://en.wikipedia.org/wiki/Henan - Economy

- Food
- Increasingly, electronics

Chongqing province (Center of China):
http://en.wikipedia.org/wiki/Chongqing - Economy

- Automobile industry (local but also overseas carmakers)

- IT (Dell, SAP)
- Finance / Banking
- Iron, steel, aluminum
- Natural resources (oil, gas, minerals)

There are of course many more provinces with factories but the ones above cover most product areas. There are also many sub-categories, which I didn't mention, because each province has a small production of nearly all product categories. You can also look at Alibaba or Global Sources and filter the supplier by province. You will see that most suppliers are in the above provinces.

Labor costs have **drastically risen in provinces like Zhejiang and Guangdong**. What used to be 250USD salary per worker in 2005 is now 1000USD or more. It is not uncommon that factories in and around the bigger cities open up a new factory further inland to lower the labor and production costs.

CHAPTER 22
WHAT TO EXPECT FROM A
SOURCING COMPANY

A sourcing company can take all your worries and headaches away. But they can also take your profits away. By saying this and making this course I am working towards unemployment myself.

Having said that it still makes sense to hire sourcing companies, especially if you don't want to deal with all the hassle and work or if you are having difficulties locating a specific supplier and monitoring your order.

Big retailers all have their own sourcing companies in Asia. Most operate on a non-profit basis, meaning these offices only charge their mother-companies a small fee to cover expenses and staff salaries. Even small importers have their buying or sourcing operations in place.

Many work in cooperation with other retailers/importers to save costs and increase order quantities through bulk purchasing, which results in lower prices.

There are thousands of Chinese sourcing companies catering to small companies but also to foreign companies that focus on western service levels. I recommend going with the latter.

Here is a rundown of the main services of a sourcing company/agent.

- **Product sourcing**

- Factory/supplier on-site verification
- Quality inspection
- Translation services
- Price negotiations
- Sample processing
- Low container consolidation
- Administrative services (flights, hotels, Visas, etc.)
- Door-to-door service

Fee structures:

- Most sourcing companies charge 5% minimum on top of the factory's price. Depending on the type of service that can be up to 30%.
- This means that the price quote you will receive from the sourcing company will already include the service fee unless stated otherwise.
- Some sourcing companies also charge an up-front fee to cover all the investment and possible time spent on working on the client's case.
- In all cases you will pay the sourcing agent when you place an order. He in turn will pay the supplier (deduct his fee) and then handle the order from there.

If you are interested in professional sourcing help you can check out the sourcing service that I offer over at: https://importdojo.com/sourcing/

CHAPTER 23
FINDING A PRODUCT IN CHINA THAT YOU SAW ON EBAY/AMAZON

I have been asked about how difficult it is to find the supplier or manufacturer of a product found on EBay, Amazon and other websites.

It can be very difficult or very easy depending on the product.

You basically have 3 options:

- **Alibaba**
- **Contacts**
- **Sourcing Agents**

Alibaba:

The key to finding the exact replica of the product you are looking for on Alibaba is keywords. Unfortunately many suppliers don't post a proper product description on Alibaba so it can be very hard to find a suitable supplier. But if it's an obvious product, it shouldn't be too difficult to find it.

Contacts:

If you have a supplier that manufactures similar or related products send him an email with a link, product descriptions, your estimated quantity, and other details you want him to know. Even if this product is not in the supplier's usual product category, you never know. As I mentioned in the *Import Bible*, suppliers are often friends with each other and they help each other too.

Send the request to all the suppliers you know. The worst that could happen is that they don't have the product.

Sourcing Agents:

Sourcing agents usually have loads of contacts and suppliers in different product categories. Bear in mind that you will pay a percentage on top of the manufacturer's price.

If you feel comfortable with that, meaning you also don't have to deal with the sourcing part, the negotiations and so on, go with the sourcing agent.

I will give you an example. In this illustration I am actually a "sourcing agent" for my client. A client of mine has asked me to look for this product:

http://www.amazon.de/BlueLotus-Wireless-LED-Blinker-Radfahren-Blinklicht-Dunkelblau/dp/B00LUHNJNW/ref=sr_1_sc_1?ie=UTF8&qid=14240 75651&sr=8-1-spell&keywords=blinkerrucksack

It's in German but you get the product idea. **The first thing** I did was to go on Alibaba since I didn't really know a supplier for this product.

I typed in "LED Vest" and got 10,660 results. Ok, I got some leads there.

When I scrolled down a little further I saw a product very similar to the one I was looking for. I looked at the supplier's website and saw that they specialize in these products. So I sent him an email with my inquiry.

Basically I was asking for a price, MOQ, delivery time and about the customers he sells this item to. Obviously I also did my routine checks on factory standards, product certifications and supplier profile. If I wanted to order from this factory later I would definitely go to see the factory. But as a first step this was sufficient.

I sent an inquiry to 3 more companies on Alibaba.

Two days later I eventually received a quotation for a product that was very similar to mine.

Milestone 1, check!

The second thing I did was to send my suppliers an inquiry, just like I sent one to the Alibaba suppliers. I think I sent it to around 10 contacts.

Within 3 days I had 2 suppliers offer me the product. One of them was exactly the product I was looking for.

Milestone 2, check!

Out of the 3 offers 2 had a similar price and 1 was way off my target price.

I confronted that supplier with the offers of the 2 other suppliers and asked him to explain his price difference.

He emailed me back and was honest enough to tell me that they are a trading company, even though initially he said they are a manufacturer.

INSIDER TIP:

Take this step to confront the supplier if you have more offers on the table. Not just to reveal the possible "middleman," but if he is an actually a manufacturer, he might give you good reasons why he is more expensive.

Perhaps it is because of a different product material, certifications or other important reasons that may be vital to your decision. Don't just brush him off if he is initially more expensive.

In this case it was really because he was a middleman, so I took my two offers from the real manufacturers and sent them to my customer. Three months later I received an order for the item.

Will the products be inferior in quality compared to the "original"?

This is a good question.

I would take the specifications of the original item (copy details from Amazon/Amazon etc.) and send them to the supplier.

If he says that he has equally good specifications I **ask him for proof.**

I would also recommend **ordering a sample of the product** that you found in China and once received, check quality and functions. Perform a simple "fit-for-use" test yourself and then decide whether you want to go ahead with this product or not.

Also remember to **calculate your costs properly**. Is your margin good enough to make you an actual profit? Because, bear in mind, you probably need to be at least 30% below the "original" product to be competitive.

Having said all this, please do not try to copy products exactly. Especially branded items. There are a lot of items out there that are "open" and can be bought regularly in the factory "off the rack." Counterfeit or copied items are simply not worth the trouble, especially if you live in a first-world country.

CHAPTER 24
MORE DROP-SHIPMENT SITES OTHER THAN ALIEXPRESS

There are of course more than the 2 usual suspects Aliexpress or Global Sources. Here is a selection of some drop-shipment online shops:

http://www.e-ville.com/en/

This is run by a Finnish guy who I personally know. They are very dedicated when it comes to service and quality. Prices are a little higher than Aliexpress but it's worth it because this guy makes sure you get your goods.

Some of the other drop-shippers that I have used or that I know of:

http://www.epathchina.com/
https://www.chinavasion.com/
http://www.tinydeal.com/
http://www.dhgate.com/
http://www.hktdc.com/suppliers/china-wholesale-suppliers/en
http://www.chinabuye.com/
http://www.china-direct-buy.com/
http://www.buychina.com/

CHAPTER 25
THE BRUTAL & HONEST TRUTH ABOUT DEVELOPING YOUR OWN PRODUCTS IN CHINA

I often receive the question on how to contact factories with your own ideas & designs. Basically, how to get a supplier manufacturer your design.

Lets say you have an idea of a completely new product or you want to modify/improve something that's already in the market.

Basically, you want to alter the design of an existing top selling product (i.e. make it better than the competition), but you aren't sure of the process to develop this modification and the potential patent laws around it.

It seems to be simple (you have a basic sketch drawn up and know it could work based on a similar mechanism used in a different, unrelated and very successful product), but you have no engineering/tooling knowledge.

Simply put, base level product that you want to alter (not just adding a logo or changing color) to make it better than the competition. How do you go on to develop this idea and get someone to manufacture it for you?

2 things you have to consider:

1. patent issues (for making existing items better)

2. finding a manufacturer without the means of funds/financial back up

1. patent issues

Lets say we are looking at a famous design from a brand. For example a fan or vaccuum clean from Dyson.

While they do have a patent on the product they also have a **registered design.**

Meaning that even you go to a factory and ask them to modify the inner components and change the design a little bit it still relies heavily on their original design.

Meaning you are in breach of their design & patent.

Now, if you are going to sell this "new" product of yours at a local shop or some street market in Thailand you probably won't have any problems.

But if you are going to sell online in your shop or for example FBA you are very likely to get in trouble with the patent or design holder.

Many factories will tell you not to worry as the design & components are slightly changed. Technically correct yes, but there is still the issue of the **"registered design"** which means that anything that has similar functions or design is inflicting the patent will have some problem.

There is no way around it. In Chinese factories it is often so obvious when they are trying to copy a big brand's product. Likely they will sell to some South East Asian country where no one cares. But lets assume you live in a first world country like the US. So you will definitely have issues.

There are patent lawyers that can check if "your product design" is inflicting any design or patent. If you are looking at a large-scale production and order I recommend doing this step. This may take weeks and cost you quite some money.

If your "idea" is completely different in terms of components and functions you don't need to worry.

2) finding a manufacturer without the means of funds/financial back up

No matter who you are speaking to about your product from the manufacturing side first you need to ask them to sign a NDA to protect yourself.

Then you should contact several suppliers that already work on similar products. You can find suppliers easily on Alibaba/Globalsources. Follow my guide on contacting suppliers there.

Once you have narrowed down the suppliers you should ask if they are interested in OEM with you. Meaning you are also willing to commit to orders and financial pre-investment.

If you have no means of financial back-up you probably won't have many chances on finding a supplier that will pre-invest for you without knowing your product idea.

Also It is very likely that if you don't sign an NDA with a factory that they "may" steal your idea.

Honestly speaking without any contacts and factories in China it is very tough for you to develop your own design. Factories will want to see orders before they start developing client's ideas. Unless you are already ordering from a factory it is difficult to ask them to make something for you.

After all they don't know you and they don't know if your product that you designed is going to sell. Say you find a factory that really believes in your product they will pre-invest for you if you allow them to sell it to other customers as well. If you want to have exclusivity you need to give written & most likely financial investment.

Why is all this? Developing a product requires a lot of tooling & engineering. Tooling's are very expensive and can take weeks to make.

Here is what you could do to get the funding for your product and contact manufacturers:

1. There are popular crowd-funding websites such as kickstarter.com or indiegogo.com that help bringing your design & idea to life. Depending on how well your campaign is running you could contact suppliers during the campaign, before or even after.

2. If you are working with offline customers such as retailers, present your ideas & design & get funding or confirmed orders from them.

My advice to this post is: start small and with products that are known to work. Work your way up in terms of order quantity and develop a private label at some point. Once you see good results in sales you should start developing your own products. At this point you will also have suppliers that you trust and that are willing to invest money in developing products for you.

CHAPTER 27
WHY YOU WILL LIKE GLOBAL SOURCES MORE THAN ALIBABA

I am so surprised that not many people know Globalsources.

I find them to be much better than Alibaba actually. Their English is better, the suppliers are much more professional, they provide amazing free services & their customer support is out of this world! I also get the feeling that there are less scammer than on Alibaba.

Lets take a look at some of their highlights:

Buyer support:

On their site there is a section with "Buyer support".

http://www.globalsources.com/SITE/BUYER-
SUPPORT.HTM?source=GSOLHP_TopNav_OS_BS

Here is a summary of what they do for you (as a registered user):

We know how important it is to find the right supplier for your business, especially when sourcing from overseas. We have compiled this library of sourcing advice (articles and videos), FAQs, surveys, monthly newsletter updates, monthly top products, and more to provide you with information to assist your preparations and decision-making when sourcing from China and Asia.

The information is collected from our in-house experts, as well as third party experts from large buying companies and import/export consultancy companies. Each of the targeted sections below will lead to individual pages for your further reading. We recommend you start with "What Every Buyer Should Know" and continue from there. Or if you have a specific question in mind, click on the "Ask The Experts" section to see if your question has already been asked/answered, and if not, go ahead and send your question direct to our experts. For general help to navigate and use our site, click on the Help/FAQ and User Guide sections.

Then there is their **"Private Sourcing Events"** section.

http://www.globalsources.com/SITE/PSE.HTM?source=GSOLHP_T opNav_OS_PSE

You can practically contact Global Sources and request to be at their next Sourcing Event as a invited Buyer. I attended one of their events in 2011 as a Buyer.

What happens is that Global Sources will ask what products you are looking for, what your quality requirements are and so on. Then they will send you a list of say 20 pre-selected suppliers within a few days and you can chose to meet with these suppliers at the said event.

Global Sources will take care of everything for you, organize to meet the selected suppliers, provide you with catalogues, quotations etc and all you need to do is come to the event.

At the event you will sit down with each supplier and discuss the suppliers products. The great thing about this is, they have been screened by Global Sources already and they know of your requirements, market etc. You don't need to explain much it's a meet & match.

Not sure which country in Asia is the best manufacturing country for your products?

Check out their **country sourcing reports** with statistics, developments & potential outside China:

http://www.chinasourcingreports.com/?source=GSOL_TopNav_MR

Also one of my all time favorites, **their Sourcing Magazines:**

http://www.globalsources.com/gsol/GeneralManager?&catalog_id=20 00000003844&design=clean&language=en&page=emag/SourcingMa gazines&src=hdr&pi_proj=10AWJP&source=GSOL_TopNav_MR

They hand pick suppliers and trending products in a lot of product categories in their magazines and its all for free!

Once you have started using Global Sources you will see what I mean.

Having said all that, Alibaba is still a giant with many products & suppliers that Global Sources cannot offer. Therefore it always makes sense to check out both websites when you are looking for a new supplier/product.

PART 3

THE IMPORT BIBLE – BUSINESS IN CHINA

BUSINESS IN CHINA

Chapter 1) Take your import to the next level, GO TO CHINA

Chapter 2) First timers guide to China and what this part is about

Chapter 3) Do's & don'ts in China

Chapter 4) Why go to China?

Chapter 5) Start your preparation

Chapter 6) Competitor research

Chapter 7) When is it even worth it?

Chapter 8) How to source for suppliers (in unusual ways / beyond Alibaba)

Chapter 9) Travel chapter (Visa, Hotels, Language etc.)

Chapter 10) Business in China

Chapter 11) At the exhibition & how to prepare

Chapter 12) At the factory

Chapter 13) After the trip

Chapter 14) Summary & 10 ways to save you money

CHAPTER 1
TAKE YOUR IMPORT TO THE NEXT LEVEL, GO TO CHINA

Hey y'all, I am heading to China!!

Yes, I mean actually getting on a plane and visiting China and its factories.

But not so fast! There are a lot of things to prepare before you go.

You should prepare for a trip that is at least 12 days long. You should visit at least 1-2 suppliers per day, and 2 days for exhibition, 2 days for travelling and 1-2 days for sightseeing. Yes, enjoy yourself a little too.

So that gives you 6 days of supplier visits, for a total of 12 potential suppliers. That would be a good number of suppliers that I would be comfortable with when I am going on a trip.

When I used to work for the buying office we did up to 4 suppliers a day.

I definitely was against that because you don't have time to sit down, discuss details and look at projects with the supplier.

When you plan a trip you need to consider:

- **The product you are sourcing for**
- **The area you are going to**
- **The relationship you have with this supplier (or not)**
- **The purpose of your trip or ultimate goal (new products,**

negotiation, new suppliers)
- Time of the year (go when there is an exhibition)
- The type of Visa you need (business or tourist)
- Hotel bookings
- Transportation

Say you want to source for lighting products. There are 2 main areas within China. One is in southern China (Guangzhou/Guzhen area) for decorative indoor lighting, the other in Zheijiang province (around Shanghai) for outdoor lighting and stainless steel products in Ningbo/Cixi.

So I would recommend going to the southern part first and then to the northern part as the southern part can be **combined with exhibitions** around Hong Kong / Guangzhou.

I go into details on where to go in the travel chapter.

This needs a lot of planning. But if you have tools and measurements in place this can be fun and easy. I would also recommend that you **start 4 months prior to your planned visit to China**, because of Visas, hotel bookings, setting up meetings with suppliers and making sure you are really prepared.

I did a few trips on a few days' notice, but that's a lot easier when you have done that a few times. Without experience I really do recommend enough time to plan.

If you plan a trip on short notice, hotels and flights can get very expensive. Not to mention that you might not be able to find a hotel during an exhibition period. Hotels that usually charge 60-80USD per night charge 400USD or more, for example, during the Canton Fair in Guangzhou.

You may also want to go to China if you have your own production running. Let me tell you, it's quite a feeling to see your own products being produced.

On top of that you can also carry out your own inspection of goods, making sure everything is up to your standards. That doesn't mean that you need to fly to China for every product production, but if you can schedule a trip around a production of yours I recommend doing so.

CHAPTER 2
FIRST TIMER'S GUIDE TO CHINA

This part is aimed at entrepreneurs who have already tested the waters of importing from China through Alibaba, an exhibition, contacts or more. If you have already started your import from China this part will take you to the next level.

I outline the most important steps to keep your business growing, what to avoid when going to China, how to communicate with suppliers at their factories, what to expect when visiting exhibitions and how to arrange meetings.

I will teach you how to negotiate contracts, travel around at virtually no cost in China, meet the real suppliers and perhaps even manufacture your own design. Sound good?

Then this is the perfect course for you to take your business to the next level.

We focus on how to make you become a professional China buyer in this course. You will also discover the best way to narrow your sourcing results without limiting your competitive advantage. You can figure out the best sourcing strategy along the way.

Parts of the course also aim to make you understand business in China, how to fit in and how you can avoid several problems, such as delays in shipment, your shipment being lost somewhere in China and making sure your factory follows the discussed topics after you leave the meeting.

I mention in Part 1 that it is essential to meet your business partner in China, be it for negotiations, to see his other products, to spy on your competition or just to get to know your partner in China.

CHAPTER 3
DOS & DON'TS IN CHINA

What are the obvious dos and don'ts in China?

DO'S

Indulge in the food

Food in China is very different from what you get back home. The Chinese food back home is "westernized" so that the average American will enjoy it.

Having said that, I personally like the food in China better. It's without all the MSG and sweet and sour sauces.

You might enjoy a Peking duck, dumplings in the south or seafood at a local restaurant. What I love most are the vegetables, especially broccoli and morning glory.

Tell your supplier when sitting down with him for food that he should choose the dishes. Just tell him that you may not be into "special things" (fish heads, pork skin, chicken feet or other things that you don't like). Don't worry; they don't serve any dogs in China anymore.

Sightseeing

Depending where your trip takes you I would recommend you to take a day or two for some sightseeing. If you are in the bigger cities like Beijing, Shanghai, Hangzhou, Guangzhou or Hong Kong, there are lots of things to see and do. Trip Advisor usually has great tips and reviews on things:

http://www.tripadvisor.com/.

Try your Chinese

It doesn't matter if you don't speak Chinese. You can learn just two words that will be much appreciated by your partner or supplier. "**Ni Hao**" meaning "Hello, how are you" and **Xie xie** meaning "thank you." People will appreciate you more if you can speak those two words.

Appreciate gifts and don't refuse them

It is very common that suppliers give gifts at the beginning or end of your meeting. Usually it would be tea or some product that may relate to the factory. Don't worry, it's not a bribe and you don't necessarily have to bring something too. It is just a little thank you for coming to visit. However, please do not refuse them, unless it's obviously a bribe or something very large that you can't fit into your suitcase. It will make your partner lose face in front of you. Gladly accept the gift with both hands open and perhaps make a nice comment.

Give out business cards with two hands

When you exchange business cards give and receive with both hands. It's an expression that pays respect.

Address people by their last name

If it's the first time meeting someone, address that person by his/her last name.

Chinese people may get offended if you address them by their first name. It's very similar in Europe. You are not "friends" yet and have not done business together, so be professional.

DON'T

Criticize China or its politics

Don't criticize China or its politics. Chinese are quite proud of their country and their accomplishments. Even if you don't agree with the country's politics, wait until your partner/supplier takes the first leap into criticizing, but even then don't overly criticize in any way.

Criticize partners/suppliers/strangers

Do not criticize someone in front of others, especially if you don't know each other well. Losing face is a very big thing in China. Also do not jokingly make remarks that could potentially upset someone. Chinese don't take western humor so well.

Be late for meetings

Chinese pay a lot of attention to being on time for meetings, picking you up somewhere or at gatherings. Try not to be too late for meetings or use it as a tactic for negotiation (making someone wait).

Touch strangers

Don't touch someone on the head, or shoulders unless you know each other very well. It makes most Chinese uncomfortable.

Be offended for very private questions (relationship status, salary etc.)

It is quite common in China to ask for one's relationship status, salary or other personal matters. Don't be offended, it is often asked in meetings. You can choose to answer or not, they won't be offended if you don't answer.

CHAPTER 4
WHY GO TO CHINA?

Honestly, there are so many reasons! Here are **8 reasons for you**:

1) You will want to see the production and how your product is being made. It's a great experience.

2) If you want to develop your own products you may want to do so in person with the factory. It may be difficult to handle through email.

Details are often misread or misunderstood in emails, especially when they are technical. A simple meeting with a supplier can solve many problems and obstacles.

3) See the real factories and not the trading companies behind Alibaba's "curtain."

4) Meet the people you have solely been dealing with over email so far. Get to know each other and perhaps even become friends. See also Chapter 3 on staying in touch and why meeting in person can be so important.

5) Get the best prices and negotiate prices one on one. Believe me, negotiating with someone face to face will get you further than any email.

Over the phone or email I have been told so many times that this is the best price they can offer. Being at the factory a few days later and convincing him in person that I need this price and his business depends on it made him agree. This also applies to claims and compensations.

Here is an example:

I remember one time when my German customer had to re-call a product from his stores and claimed the factory owed him 40,000USD. That was obviously an almost impossible task through email for me. There is not much I (or you) can do from an office 1000 miles away from the factory. I knew that my customer was asking for too much and that he would be happy with 5,000USD. To start I sent the supplier an email and explained the situation. I didn't have much evidence from the customer either, apart from an email and some back up material. For weeks the supplier wouldn't agree to any compensation.

So I eventually flew up to Ningbo to talk to him under the pretense of expanding business. We met up, discussed new potential products, and eventually I mentioned the claim. I told him I am not leaving until we have a solution. So eventually around 11 pm that night he agreed after hours of talking (he actually left for 1 hour in between) to a compensation of 20,000USD. And not just to be deducted from the next order but a telegraphic bank transfer within the next 2 days to the customer's bank account.

You can imagine how happy my customer was because he didn't expect anything at all, knowing he was thousands of miles away and couldn't do much.

How did I achieve that? "Simply" by meeting up with the supplier face to face. Ok, obviously if you are based far away and you have no means of travelling to the factory for a discussion like that it's going to be difficult. But you get my point.

6) Become an expert in your products and understand even technical specifications that your customers will love you for. If you want to stand out in today's competition you need to be an expert. When you sit at a meeting with your potential customer and you are confident with your products and company's ideals, it will give you an edge over your competition. No one but the manufacturer can explain his product as good as he can.

7) Take the time to visit another country and get new ideas. Apart from seeing new products and ideas at exhibitions and factories you can also get inspired by trends. Remember Chapter 6 in the *Import Bible*. Travelling is a great means to get inspired by trends in other countries.

8) Last but not least you will want to go to Yiwu. Where is that? It's a "small city" near Ningbo (Zhejiang province) that houses "The World's Largest Wholesale Market." Here is a report from Business Insider. It would definitely be worth going there, especially if you don't have many supplier contacts yet or there is no exhibition at the time of your trip.

http://www.businessinsider.com/yiwu-china-largest-wholesale-market-2011-10?op=1#ixzz3V5meL6e8

Going to China can be quite an experience and there are many reasons to make the trip.

I have heard from buyers that it's dreadful for them to go to China.

Well, it's certainly a different culture and there are many differences from the western world, be it the food, the people, the traffic jams or the bureaucracies.

But if you follow this guide I can guarantee you that you can make your trip comfortable and most of all, successful, and you'll want to go back!

What's more, you will have fun during your trip and perhaps enjoy a cup of tea somewhere in Hangzhou or sip a cocktail in the world's highest bar in Hong Kong. China has its perks and I hope you will discover them.

CHAPTER 5
START YOUR PREPARATION

Once you decide you want to go to China, take a notepad and write a few things down you will want to cover on your trip. Here are some examples on what you need to consider:

Am I seeing my existing suppliers?

If so, you should prepare yourself for that. Print out all price sheets, quotes, or topics that you would like to discuss with your supplier.

Put it in your "trip-book" (see later chapter). Is there an ongoing negotiation or claim you would like to discuss? Make sure you have all details with you that will come in handy when talking to your supplier.

Shopping list:

When I go on a sourcing trip I prepare a "shopping list" for the supplier and myself.

It's a simple Excel file (you can use the one in the supporting docs of this website and I'll give you an example below).

I input ideas I find on the Internet or at competitor's websites and send them to all my suppliers before I go on a trip. Hopefully they send back some offers of items or even samples before I go there. Then, once I am there I don't need to look any further but to the meeting room in the factory and I can discuss the products one by one. Here is what a shopping list may look like:

Item	Picture	Version	MOQ	FOB	Comparison items	Comparison price	Comments
KISSABLE		2200mAH			http://www.amazon.co.uk/ RETOUCH-POWER-KISSABLE-Lipstick-Smartphone/dp/B00NLDR5KO		
BLUSH		2100mAH			http://www.ebay.com/itm/ Blush-Make-up-Power-Bank charger-4200mAh-Battery-iPad-air-mini-4-3-2-case-cable-/151476045206		
BLUSH		4200mAH			http://www.ebay.com/itm/ Blush-Make-up-Power-Bank charger-4200mAh-Battery-iPad-air-mini-4-3-2-case-cable-/151476045206		
FUNK		Bluetooth			http://www.lazada.co.th/ed ifier-bluetooth-mp260-yellow-253232.html		
KITT		Bluetooth			http://www.lazada.co.th/im ported-smartwatches-u8-red-729963.html		
TRAINER		Bluetooth			http://www.lazada.co.th/im ported-zgpax-s28-154-inch-capacitive-touch-screen-gsm-watch-phone-black-silver-1-free-j5-in-ear-style earphone-467190.html		
BT-19		Bluetooth			http://www.lazada.co.th/jte sports-bt-517815.html		

Am I looking at new potential suppliers?

If you are unhappy with your products or your current supplier you may want to look at a new supplier to discuss your terms. Look in this course and the *Import Bible* on how to find new suppliers.

Are the flights for my dates within the budget and available?

Most flights to China from anywhere in the world range from 800-1500USD.

Check on your preferred website for booking flights or your travel agent for your desired dates. I usually use flight-search engines like www.

Once I find the cheapest flight I go onto the airline's website directly. Often times the flights there are cheaper if I book directly with the airline. This also allows free changes while most agents will charge you a fee to change a flight.

Check if there is a direct flight to your desired city. Many airlines around the world have a direct (or 1 stop) flight to your final destination.

> **Tip:** The preferred and most economical way of course would be coach/economy class. But often people don't even look at business class (or premium economy). I often find flights that are only 200-300USD more than economy. If that were the case I would definitely book business class. That way I get to arrive fresh and probably sleep a few hours while I wouldn't in economy. That's also probably because I am very tall and on top of that scared of flying (especially in economy).

Are there any Chinese holidays when I will be there?

Also see Part 1 of this eBook. Check if there are any holidays when you are scheduled to be there. Otherwise you might end up going and find that everything is closed.

Which products am I looking for this time?

Do you have new product ideas that you want to discuss or do you want to enlarge your assortment with similar products? Bring samples of your new products, print outs or your shopping list as support.

Which area am I going to?

Depending on your product you might want to fly directly to the nearest largest city where you have a base for the trip. Many carriers fly directly from Europe or the US to large cities like Guangzhou, Shanghai, Beijing and Hong Kong.

How can I travel between suppliers and exhibitions or meetings?

I will go into detail later but my preferred way of travelling within China is by car, usually provided by the supplier. If I go from Hong Kong to Guangzhou or Shenzhen, though, I take the train.

The purpose or ultimate goal of my trip

What is the ultimate goal of my trip? Write yourself a to-do list and what goals you want to achieve. While on your trip, keep looking at the list and remind yourself of your goals.

The type of Visa you need

There are many types of Visas but the most common ones are tourist or business Visas. I will go into detail in the travel section.

What's my hotel budget?

Hotels in China are very cheap and ultra-modern compared to the western world. The big names and 5 star hotels like Marriot, Hilton, Crowne Plaza, etc., can go for as little as 70USD per night. That is off-season and not in the big cities like Shanghai, Hong Kong and Guangzhou. But there are many Asian 5-star chains that are equally good and are cheaper. More on that in the travel section.

Prepare prices & raw material costs for negotiation

Print out raw material costs that you can find on the Internet. This might help you during a negotiation when someone claims an increase of raw material prices.

CHAPTER 6
COMPETITOR RESEARCH

This is an **essential part** of your trip, to research a product that your competition has that you don't have or to make sure that your ideas aren't already showing up everywhere.

Know your competition! Since you started your business, have you done research on your competition?

What do they already have in their shop/store that you don't?

How can you get this product and perhaps even have a better one?

Take a few hours of your week and look at your competitor's websites. Search for new products or announcements.

Subscribe to their email newsletter (use a email other than your work email) and get their latest products into your inbox.

You will also want to take the ideas and new products from your competition with you on your trip. Print information about the products out and put them in your trip book (the trip book is explained in a later chapter).

Send your suppliers your competitor's products (perhaps in a shopping list) and ask them if they have **something similar or even more advanced**. This saves you a lot of time because by the time you get to China you may already have a sample on the meeting table that is similar or even better than your competitor's product. (See also the previous chapter regarding preparation.)

CHAPTER 7
WHEN IS IT WORTH IT TO GO TO CHINA?

If you have read the *Import Bible* and you are absolutely comfortable with the ways you are importing then you probably shouldn't be going. Perhaps you aren't ready yet either. Business is going well and you need more time to focus on sales rather than purchasing. That's fine.

But if you feel that you are stuck with price negotiations, have had a bad experience with existing suppliers, want to see some trends at exhibitions or look at your competitor's production **then** you should be going to China.

When you haven't done business directly with Chinese factories then you can't know for sure if this is going to bring your business forward.

When you meet someone face to face it's a completely different relationship. Your and your supplier will have more trust with each other. What's more, Chinese hospitality is actually very open and welcoming.

Many times during a meeting in a factory there are situations where you can learn a lot about your competition. Either the supplier gives away some vital information about trends or you can actually find a gift box of your toughest competitor's in the production line.

Or perhaps you see production for a company that you don't know but it could be your potential next customer? Take a snapshot and do some research later.

All these things cannot be done through email or phone calls from the comfort of your home. You need to see them.

CHAPTER 8
HOW TO SOURCE FOR SUPPLIERS (IN UNUSUAL WAYS / BEYOND ALIBABA)

This chapter is dedicated to finding suppliers in an unusual way, beyond Alibaba. There are a few ways to find suppliers that I am going to elaborate on now:

Taobao

Taobao is the equivalent to EBay and Amazon based in China. It belongs to the Alibaba group. You will need to speak and read Chinese if you want to communicate with the suppliers.

Actually most people on there are not suppliers but private persons, similar to EBay sellers.

If you are using Google Chrome you can auto-translate the site but be aware that the translation might not be accurate.

You can, however, find some great products and ideas if you auto-translate the site and its categories. You can browse through categories and if you see something that you like on there you could send it to your supplier and ask if he has any knowledge of this product and where to find it.

There are many items on there that you won't find on Aliexpress or Alibaba/Globalsources, mainly because these items are created for the Chinese market and taste.

BUT, you can find items or trends in China on there that could very well work in your country too. Remember, country specific trends could be your next great idea (see the *Import Bible* on ways to product sourcing).

Global sources magazine

I mentioned this already in the *Import Bible*. Global Sources provides a magazine that lists suppliers and their products.

I am really astonished on how little people know about this service. They usually update every category every few weeks/months. The content is amazing. High quality photos, descriptions, supplier details, trends, everything!

It's a great way of getting ideas and finding suppliers.

Have a look here and take a look at the many different product groups that they cover:

http://www.globalsources.com/gsol/GeneralManager?&catalog_id=200 0000003844&design=clean&language=en&page=emag/SourcingMaga zines&src=hdr&pi_proj=10AWJP&source=GSOLHP_TopNav_MR

Another great services by Global Sources:

You can actually contact Global Sources and ask them anything for free (as long as you are registered). If you are looking for a product or a supplier of a specific product, maybe even in a specific area, they can help find it.

Check it out:

http://www.globalsources.com/SITE/BUYER-SUPPORT.HTM?source=GSOLHP_TopNav_OS_BS

Exhibitor's lists

I also mentioned this in the *Import Bible* already. You can look at and find suppliers from exhibitions even you if you haven't attended.

Then click on **"Full Exhibitor List"** and there you go. You have all exhibitors exhibiting at this fair. It's a bit of a lengthy process but you can check all websites of the suppliers, look at their products, and contact them directly without even going to the exhibition.

This applies to almost any exhibition in the world.

By the way, this is also a great way to find potential CUSTOMERS.

If you are planning to sell to retailers or wholesalers you can also look at these exhibitor's lists and see them as a potential sales lead.

Baidu search

Baidu is the most used search engine in China (since Google is blocked). Everything is in Chinese, but just like Taobao you can auto-translate the page.

I use it sometimes to look for a specific product. It's like a supplier directory, listing a lot of suppliers. For example, if you type "handbag manufacturer" you will find mostly results that lead to Chinese companies. A few overseas websites are listed too but not as many as if you would use Google.

Baidu can also help you to find patents on items that you may be looking for.

Baidu has a separate website for that, called Baidu Zhuanli: http://zhuanli.baidu.cn/

Again, you can translate via auto-translate but it is very difficult to navigate if you don't read/speak Chinese. You can ask your supplier to check it for you.

How to find local fairs & wholesale markets

Apart from finding the big exhibitions that I mentioned under Part 1 in the *Import Bible*, there are many other exhibitions or wholesale markets that may be worth looking at. At many of those markets the MOQ can be quite low, so this might be an ideal starting point for you.

Prices are usually a little more expensive than from the factory since many of the companies there are trading companies or agents for factories.

Many cities in China have an "exhibition center" that houses all-year exhibitions or wholesale markets. Here is a list of some of the biggest wholesale markets/all year exhibitions in China:

The most famous one, housing everything from electronics to toothbrushes is in Yiwu.

YIWU MARKET:

http://www.businessinsider.com/yiwu-china-largest-wholesale-market-2011-10?op=1#ixzz3V5meL6e8
http://en.wikipedia.org/wiki/Yiwu_market

Clothing wholesale markets:

Guangzhou Baima market
www.baima.com
Address: 16 Zhannan Rd Guangzhou Guangdong Province

Humen Fumin Fashion City
www.fumin.com
Address: Humen Town, Dongguan City, Guangdong Province

Hangzhou Sijiqing apparel wholesale market
Over 1200 manufacturers with stores at this market. There is an annual sale of 6billion RMB reported from this market.
Address: 31-59 Hanghai Rd Hangzhou Zhejiang province

Furniture wholesale markets:

Shunde furniture wholesale market
The largest furniture wholesale market in China. It's actually 1 mall after another on that road. You could drive for 15 minutes along that road and you will still find showrooms of factories.
http://en.wikipedia.org/wiki/Shunde,_China_Furniture_Wholesale_Market

Electronics wholesale markets:

Shenzhen SEG Electronics Wholesale Market
This market is China's largest electronics market and sits in between Shennan Road and North Huaqing road. It is located at the SEG plaza and occupies the first to the tenth floors. The market has over 3000 shops.

Address: Intersection of Mid Shennan Rd and North Huaqiang Rd, Shenzhen

http://en.wikipedia.org/wiki/SEG_Plaza

Shenzhen Huaqiang Electronics World (HEW)

This market is China's second largest electronics market and covers many categories.

There are 2800 stores that specialize in electronics and computers.

Address: No 1007—No 1015 North Huaqiang Rd, Shenzhen, Guangdong

Guangzhou Electronics Wholesale Market (GEC)

Guangzhou Electronics City (GEC) is a large-scale market that specializes in electrical equipment. It is located on the first floor of a newly built exhibition center that is to the west of the Guangzhou Cultural Park on Xidi Second Road. With more than 6000 m2 business area and over 300 independent stores, it covers communication equipment, fax machines, telephones and various audio and photography equipment, as well as game consoles and other small electrical appliances.

Address: No 94 Liwan Rd, Guangzhou

Toys wholesale market:

Guangzhou International Toys & Gifts Centre

Located in the Guangzhou Huangpu International Logistics Park, the Guangzhou International Toys and Gifts Centre (GITGC), with 1.5 billion total investments, covers a total construction area of 320 thousand square meters, which makes it the largest toy and gift distribution center nationwide.

There are nearly 800 shops that are mainly in the form of street shops. Address: F14 West Tower, Shangjian Bldg, No66 Huacheng Ave, Zhujiang Xincheng, Guangzhou.

Beijing International Toys City (BITC)

Beijing International Toys City (BITC) has over 1000 shops. You will find famous domestic and international brands of toys of all kinds such as electronics, plush toys, woodwork, handicraft gifts, etc.
Address: No 67 South Third Ring Rd

China Toys & Amusement Facilities Wholesale Market

China Toys and Amusement Facilities Wholesale Market sits in Tianjia Wan of east Xianning Road in Xi'an. The market is divided into five areas, namely toys and children's articles, amusement facility wholesale, electric toys wholesale, fitness appliance wholesale and arts and crafts wholesale. There are approximately 300 stores.
Address: No 188 Tianjia Wan, East Xianning Rd, Xi'an.

CHAPTER 9
TRAVEL CHAPTER

1. Travel preparations
2. Which area do I go to?
3. How to book and how to cancel hotels
4. Lowdown on what to expect in China in terms of lack of English
5. Basic Visa overview
6. The trip book
7. What to pack
8. How to travel within China

1) Travel Preparations – The Essentials

When I plan a trip for a buyer or for myself to check out factories I go through the following checklist:

- Do I look for new products or do I want to negotiate existing items/contracts?
- What products am I sourcing for?
- Which area do I need to go to for these? (Alibaba filtering by product/province)
- Do I have supplier contacts for these products or do I need to source for them first?
- How many days do I want to go?
- When do I want to go?
- Can I combine the trip with an exhibition?

- Can someone take care of my daily business back home? (Be reminded Google and Gmail will not work in China so you can't check your Gmail.)

2) Which area do I go to?

Based on your products you can figure out which area you need to go to. Main airline carriers sometimes flythrough directly to big cities like Guangzhou, Hong Kong, Shanghai and Beijing these days.

3) How to book and how to cancel hotels

I usually use www.agoda.com for my hotel bookings. First off you get reward points that you can later use for free rooms (or for a discount on your bookings) and secondly I find that they usually have the cheapest rates out there.

There are a few price comparison websites out there such as www.tripadvisor.com.

You can also look at www.hotels.com or www.booking.com to compare the rates.

Sometimes I also ask my supplier if he has any special rate for a hotel nearby his factory. Suppliers often get great rates (that you won't find anywhere on the Internet) because they send hotels a lot of customers. For example, I have 1 supplier in Ningbo who can get me a rate at the Ningbo Marriot for 650RMB while the rate online is 1080RMB and through travel agencies it would be 900RMB.

If you don't feel comfortable booking online or through your supplier then ask your local travel agency, but I have found they are usually more expensive.

Print out your booking confirmation, as you may need it for check in or to show it to a driver (or taxi) who picks you up at the airport. The booking confirmation often has the local address in the local language.

Insider's tip:

If you aren't sure about your trip and itinerary yet book through www.agoda.com.

Why? Some of their rooms online can be cancelled 7 days before arrival without a charge. **Why is that important?**

When you apply for your China Visa you need to provide flight and hotel booking information upon application. So even if you aren't going to stay at a certain place you can book it for now and cancel it later after you have your Visa.

Hotels during the exhibition

Book a hotel now if you haven't booked it yet!

Hotels can get quite expensive during the exhibition periods, especially Hong Kong and Guangzhou hotels. What's more, hotels could easily be booked up during these periods.

When you book a hotel try to be close by a subway, train station or airport for convenient travelling.

Hotel tips in large cities

When I worked for a large retailer we usually stayed in a 5 star hotel with prices up to 150$. But if I wanted to save money a 4 star hotel in China is equally good as a 5 star hotel overseas and they go for 60$.

Here are a few hotel options. Most of them are at a reasonable price off-season and ideally located to where I needed to go.

$$$ - Plush/luxury
$$ - Mid range / business hotel
$ - Budget

Shenzhen

Shangri-La $$$

This hotel is within walking distance to the Hong Kong border and at a reasonable price. Ideal when you want to leave early morning to the factories or go for some shopping at the nearby mall.

Best Western $$

Also ideally located next to the train station. Convenient to get around.

Guangzhou

Garden Hotel $$$

Expensive but very nice rooms and excellent breakfast buffet. Not far from the most important spots.

The Landmark $$

This is my favorite hotel in Guangzhou as prices are extremely competitive during the exhibitions and it's right next to a Metro line that takes me all the way to the Canton Fair.

Lavande Hotel $

Budget hotel I stayed in on my last trip during Canton Fair. Ok for 1 or 2 nights.

Hangzhou

Shangri-La $$$
Very nice rooms and ideally located. Too expensive for my taste but nice.

Citadines $
Almost budget hotel. Good location and easy to get around.

Ningbo

Ningbo Marriot $$$
Expensive for Ningbo but still affordable. Great location and excellent restaurant.

Howard Johnson $$
Not far from the CBD and very affordable.

Crown Plaza $$
Great location, the food is so-so.

Cixi

Cixi Hangzhou Bay Hotel $$
Very nice location, the back yard looks onto the mountains. Food is ok for the area but not much of a selection.

Shanghai

The Langham Shanghai Xintiandi $$$
Very expensive but in the middle of Xiantiandi, great for a stroll at night.

Pullman Shanghai Skyway $$

Inexpensive, location ok and a nice bar on the top floor.

Hotel Equatorial Shanghai $$

I usually stayed in this hotel in Shanghai during my trips. Great price, nice rooms and OK food.

Beijing

Park Hyatt Beijing Hotel $$$

Very nice hotel, but also very expensive. Great location.

Four Seasons Hotel Beijing $$$

Similar to the Park Hyatt, but a little less expensive.

Traders Hotel Beijing By Shangri-La $$

Affordable and great location.

Novotel Peace Beijing Hotel $$

Great location, great food, easy to reach.

Radisson BLU Hotel $$

Heavily Asian themed but rooms are ok.

Swissotel Beijing Hong Kong Macau Center Hotel $$

Very nice and great prices.

Dongguan

Sheraton Dongguan Hotel $$$

Great food and excellent location.

Mels Weldon Dongguan Humen $$

Stunning rooms for a great price. Excellent Teppaniaki restaurant attached.

Grand Mercure Dongguan Humen By Accor $$

Excellent prices and rooms.

Shunde

Sheraton $$

Large buffet selection and great rooms.

Hong Kong (based on my buyers)

Shangri La Kowloon East $$$

Pricey but excellent rooms and food. Many restaurants nearby.

Intercontinental Kowloon East $$$

Great sea view rooms, next to the harbor.

The Royal Pacific $$

On Canton Road where all the big brand shops are located. Great for a walk at the park or a stroll down to the Star Ferry.

iClub $$

On Hong Kong Island, ideally located in Sheung Wan (next to Central) and 4 minute walk to the metro line (MTR).

4) What to expect in China in terms of lack of English

Pretty much everyone speaks English these days, especially representatives of factories or staff at hotels. Your main concern when it comes to non-English speaking people would be taxi drivers, staff at train stations or local restaurants.

Make sure that you carry around your hotel's name card or booking confirmation with the address in Chinese on it.

If you are out on your own for sightseeing bring a map from the hotel or ask your supplier to give you a few tips on what to see and not get lost.

There are also inexpensive Chinese language books you can buy back home to bring along the way. They often have the most common phrases that might come in handy at the back of the book (Marco Polo, Lonely Planet, etc.).

Your factory contact should be able to speak proper English. More on that in a later section.

5) Basic Visa overview

Visa

Visitors to Mainland China need to obtain a Visa from their country's consulate to China. Visas can be issued for up to 30 days, depending on your passport. Here is a Wikipedia excerpt:

http://en.wikipedia.org/wiki/Visa_policy_of_China

To look up what Visa you need for China you can go onto Wikipedia and then click on your country's link. You will be redirected to your Visa requirements for all countries, based on your nationality.

Most of my buyers usually applied for a **business Visa**. That's because it was an official business trip from a large company. To do so, you need an **invitation letter** from your supplier that states that he is inviting you to China to do business. This can be a simple letter that your supplier can draft for you.

A business Visa usually takes 4-7 days, depending on your passport.

You need to apply for it at your local embassy to China.

For individuals who come to China for the first time I recommend you apply for a **tourist Visa**. A tourist Visa allows you to stay up to 30 days and you can travel within China as you like. Most first-timers use this type of Visa as it's easy to attain and no one will know if you are doing business or just sightseeing. You need to apply for it at your local embassy to China.

Tourist Visas can generally be done within 7-10 days, depending on which one you need.

If you are going to the south of China (Guangzhou) you can also get a **Visa on arrival** in Shenzhen (border to Hong Kong) for 3 days. You can only use this Visa within Shenzhen, but they don't need to know you are going to Guangzhou after your entry. Just don't depart through any other border than the one you entered.

This Visa on arrival also applies now in 13 other bigger cities within China:

http://www.travelchinaguide.com/embassy/Visa/free-72hour/

If you are one of the qualifying countries from the list you can stay up to 72 hours within the city of arrival. However, you may not exit through any other immigration point other than the one you entered through.

China Visas issued in Hong Kong are also an easy way to get a Visa.

There are many providers for this kind of service in Hong Kong. This one here is the most widely used provider:

https://www.ctshk.com/english/useful/chineseVisa.htm

They can be found everywhere around HK, at the airport, train stations, subway stations, etc. You give them your passport and depending on how fast you want your Visa, they can sometimes do it in a day. It gets more expensive the faster you want it, obviously.

Type of entry:

Single
Double
Multiple

Most visitors will only be issued a **single entry** into China, especially for tourist Visas. That means once you exit China you need to apply for a new Visa.

Double entry Visas will only be issued for **a business Visa**.

If you have previously been to China you can apply for a **multiple entry Visa** that usually lasts 6 or 12 months. You can come and go as many times as you want within the given time frame. This Visa is usually only issued for business Visas and if you have had a double entry Visa issued before.

Conclusion:

If you are planning a single trip to China for a few days, not leaving the country, for example Hong Kong/Taiwan, and planning to come back I recommend you apply for a tourist Visa. If you are going on a trip that requires you to enter and exit China at least once, I recommend you apply for a business Visa.

Here is a scenario: you plan to visit an exhibition in Hong Kong, and then head to China for factory visits or an exhibition. You then come back to Hong Kong and leave Asia through Hong Kong.

You can apply for your Visa back in your home country or on the day of arrival in Hong Kong. **BUT** note that you need to have **at least 2-3 days within Hong Kong** before you can get your Visa (unless you opt for the expensive express service). Once you have received your Visa in your passport (for example single entry tourist Visa) you can go to China via train or plane. Make sure you book a return ticket for your Visa application.

6) The trip book

You **definitely want to make yourself one**. It will come in handy, trust me.

So what is the trip book and what does the trip book include?

Basically it's a small binder map that I make myself with all necessary documents and prepared material.

Print out the following and put it in there:

- Hotel reservations
- Flight bookings
- Addresses of the hotels and factories that you are going to.
- Price sheets of offers from suppliers (who knows, your laptop might die on you).
- Your own company presentation / flyer / catalogue.
- Prepare yourself a small introduction of your company (perhaps a PowerPoint presentation) that you can print out and show the supplier.
- Supplier profile sheet (I provide an example sheet in the supporting documents available in my ImportDojo Masterclass: https://importdojo.com/importdojo-masterclass/
- Raw material price sheets
- Shopping list
- *Import Bible*

You want the suppliers to be professional so be professional yourself.

If you can, print the e-book of this course, so you can look up something if you forget.

7) What to pack:

First, what time of the year is it? It can get pretty hot from April-October and very cold in winter, especially in the factories as there is usually no heating.

Here is a list of what I pack when on a trip:

- Travel adaptor
- The trip book
- Laptop / tablet
- Business cards
- Warm clothes
- Business attire (you wouldn't want to be greeted in shorts and a t-shirt either)
- Casual attire, for those strolls along the Bund in Shanghai or the Star Ferry ride in Hong Kong.
- Passport
- Pens and paper or notebooks
- Power packs to charge your electronic smart-devices
- Chinese money (Renminbi-Yuan), but not too much, as withdrawing from the ATM in China is cheaper than exchanging at banks/airports or at home

8) How to travel within China

My preferred way of travelling is by car. There is a great train network within China but it can be a hassle to get tickets and you will be surrounded by hundreds of people in the train. If I travel by car (from the supplier) I get to work on my laptop in peace and I am taken straight to the door of my next appointment.

Travel for FREE within China (almost)

I almost never pay for anything when I travel within China apart from the flight or hotel costs.

How do I do that?

Simply ask your supplier to pick you up at a specific place (your hotel) and bring you to another place. I have never had a supplier who refused to pick me up or bring me somewhere, even if I didn't have business with him (yet).

When I look at my schedule I will give my first supplier my pick-up address. I will also give him the address of my second appointment. This way, the supplier can take me to the next address after the meeting. I then advise my second appointment of my estimated arrival time and tell him where my third appointment is that he should take me to after our meeting.

You can also give your second appointment the address of the first appointment but you never know how long your first appointment may take. So it's better your first appointment has the address of your second appointment. If I have more than 2 appointments in a day I repeat this step for each supplier until the last one, who I will ask to bring me back to the hotel or airport.

To be safe you should also ask your first appointment how far the second appointment is from his factory. Generally I would say that most factories are 1 ½ hours away from each other. So plan accordingly.

I also give each supplier the telephone number of my previous and next appointment, just in case the driver gets lost and needs to call my next appointment for directions.

I use this tactic also with suppliers when I land at the airport.

I will ask my first appointment supplier to pick me up at the airport and bring me to the hotel, even if the appointment is the next day. I will be seeing them during the trip and they are usually happy to pick me up and have a quick chat in the car before they drop me off at the hotel.

Most suppliers will provide me a car for a distance not further than 200 kilometers from their factory. If a distance is further than that I use trains or planes.

Air tickets will obviously be on my expense account but this way I save train tickets or taxi fees. It also gives me time to chat with the supplier in the car or to work on my notes from my previous meeting.

CHAPTER 10
BUSINESS IN CHINA / OEM / PRIVATE LABEL ETC.

- Finding translators, evaluating translators
- Do's and don'ts of dealing with Chinese, business culture, appearance, and customs
- What to expect and a small guide of common situations (supplier invites you to eat... and so on)
- OEM
- NDA (Non-disclosure agreement)

Finding translators, evaluating translators

The question actually is, do you need one, because most people speak English, especially your factory's sales contact.

In my 10 years in Asia I didn't need to learn the Chinese language. That doesn't mean I didn't learn it but I was fine in the first few years without it.

When you constantly have someone from the factory to help you, you don't need a translator. And honestly if no one at the factory speaks some English I wouldn't even recommend working with that factory. Just imagine how difficult it will be to process an order with him if he doesn't speak basic English. You might as well skip the "translator" part.

There are times when a person who speaks Chinese comes in handy, such as when the factory sends you off with a driver to your next meeting or hotel. But in that case you should always have the mobile number and address in Chinese of your previous or your next meeting's contact.

If I look at my statistics throughout travelling to China within the last 10 years (being stationed in Hong Kong), I was not once stuck somewhere that I needed a translator. If my English can get me through and I am not native, then so will your English.

It's a different situation if your English is not as good as you would want it to be. Then I would recommend you find a translator. Honestly I never used a translator so I don't have any good references. Translators are very easy to find though on Google or even Alibaba.

Often times you will find Chinese people waiting in front of exhibition centers to offer their translation services. Don't hire them. You really don't need them. Again, most staff of factories will speak English at a level that is sufficient for your business.

Dos and don't's of dealing with Chinese, business culture, appearance, and customs

It is rather common that when you meet with a supplier the first thing they ask is if you **want to eat**. They simply don't want you to be hungry it seems.

I don't travel for fun and food but for business. So usually when I have a tight schedule I will politely ask for some fast food to order while we have the meeting. Often times they will want to go for lunch or dinner with you after a meeting.

Most of the time it takes about 1½ hour to go from one meeting to another, so I usually decline lunches as my day is normally packed with meetings with other suppliers. Your supplier won't be offended, just explain that you have a packed day of meetings and that you would be happy to have a meal another day.

If you do find the time to have lunch or dinner go for it. Mostly the supplier pays for it but you should offer to pay for your share or the entire meal. But again, in 99% of the cases he will not let you pay for the meal/dinner anyway.

It is also common that suppliers will present you **with a gift** before or after your meeting. Usually it is some tea, a tie or some small inexpensive gift. It is expected of you to take it. You don't have to bring gifts but if you have some inexpensive gift as well it sure is a nice way to treat your supplier.

When I go to meetings within China I usually wear a suit and a shirt. I wear suits because they are comfortable to wear and sit in. You don't have to wear a full suit and tie, as it is not expected of you. But I recommend you to wear long pants and a long-sleeve shirt or a polo shirt. You will want to **have a professional image** in front of the supplier. I wouldn't take a buyer seriously if he showed up in shorts and a t-shirts.

When you meet your supplier for the first time, **name cards and basic pleasantries will be exchanged**. After that you usually get to the subject or issue on hand. There is no need to have hours of small talk. Just get to the point, be precise and make notes of what was discussed.

It is quite common that the supplier will sometimes ask you very personal things like income or relationship status. Don't be alarmed; it is simply their way of showing interest in you.

OEM

I explained OEM in the *Import-Bible* already. OEM stands for "original equipment manufacturer" and it means that you have your (or your clients) own design that you will want your supplier to manufacture for you exclusively.

OEM products are **usually not showcased** on a manufacturer's website/exhibition or even showroom. The manufacturer is not allowed to show it to customers other than you.

The advantage of OEM is that you alone own the design, and no one else can.

The disadvantage is that there is a lot of pre-investment involved. I recommend this option only if you have the available funds/backup (for example, from crowd-sourcing website Kickstarter.com) or if you are willing to invest in it yourself because you strongly believe in your design.

When does it make sense to manufacture OEM?

If you are not in a niche and you have many competitors you will want to stand out.

Selling items off-the-rack works just fine in the beginning but if you want to take your business to the next level you will want to introduce new and unique products to your clients.

Most factories will advertise in their first email "welcome for OEM business," While the actual truth is no factory will immediately agree to do OEM with you without having established any business. Their first intention is to sell you their existing items as OEM involves a lot of planning and financing.

Depending on your product, OEM usually requires a larger up-front order quantity to cover the tooling and development costs. This applies to products that need some sort of mold or tool. Textiles or other one-part products can be made at lower quantities. Prices for tooling can start at 8000USD and go up to 50,000USD.

If you have a design or prototype it makes sense to discuss it with your supplier and figure out the costs that are involved. Factories usually have an engineering department that can calculate costs involved. The supplier will then usually give you a price that covers all costs or he may offer you a lower price and add an extra charge for the tooling.

NDA

OEM should also cover a non-disclosure-agreement (NDA) with your supplier, prohibiting him and any of his employees from discussing your designs, prototypes or product developments.

It is vital that you have an NDA agreement with a supplier if you work with him for a long time and if you are discussing exclusive product developments.

Suppliers are usually ok with signing an agreement.

You never know, an NDA agreement can come in handy if you need to deal with lawyers or lawsuits.

I provide a sample NDA agreement under supporting documents here: https://importdojo.com/importdojo-masterclass/

CHAPTER 11
AT THE EXHIBITION & HOW TO PREPARE

Here is what I bring to exhibitions:

- Name cards (an absolute MUST)
- Trolley to carry all the catalogues that I collect
- My own (printed) company presentation
- Notebook & pens
- Passport photo (some exhibitions such as the Canton fair require a passport photo)
- Comfortable shoes (you will be walking all day)

How to register?

Most exhibitions require you to pre-register if you want to get in for free.

All you need to do is look up the exhibition's website and there will be an area or link where you can fill in your application.

Registration on-site is also possible but usually there will be a fee of 10-20USD. You will need to provide a name card for your registration.

When you pre-register online, just fill in your company's details and print out the confirmation. Bring that confirmation and you will be handed a badge for entry.

The Canton Fair has the same procedure, however you can keep your badge for years to come. If you lose your badge you will have to pay a fee of 200RMB for re-issuance. There is a first time registration fee of 100RMB. If you have a supplier who can invite you, you don't need to pay any fees. Also remember to bring along a passport photograph for the application (required).

You can register here, among other useful tools for the Canton Fair:

http://invitation.cantonfair.org.cn/en/

Remember to keep the badge for the Canton Fair, as it is valid for years to come.

How to act and ask questions at exhibitions

I usually prepare a little speech before I go to the exhibition. It depends on my project or product that I am looking for but I like to introduce myself a little bit and give the supplier a professional image of me.

He is likely more interested in giving me answers, good prices or proper email feedback after the exhibition. Here is how it could look:

Hi, I am Manuel and I am the Managing Director of Mandarin-Gear Limited in Hong Kong.

I manage/own a sourcing and buying office for many large retailers worldwide.

My customers are looking for product "X" and I am interested in discussing more details or receiving a quotation based on my customer's requirements.

Then I ask my questions and once I am satisfied I will ask him to provide me a quote based on my requirements. I will hand him my business card and I will **MAKE SURE** that he wrote down everything we discussed.

Could you please send me a quote of this item (from his booth) based on "X" quantity, including certification "XY"?

I will also take his name card and catalogue to study later.

Here are some questions that I ask the suppliers. You can adapt these to your product or requirements as necessary. You can also make yourself a checklist with these questions and print it out for each supplier meeting you have.

Obviously you can also memorize these questions and make notes on your notepad.

Clip the supplier's name card to your notebook and write down answers to these questions:

- **When was his factory established?**

  This is important as to figure out if he has been doing business for a long time or if he is newly established. If the factory is brand new I will be wary of dealing with them, while if they are older than 5 years I will probably go ahead with further questions.

- **What is the total count of staff, workers, engineers and managers?**

  A well-organized factory has at least 200 employees. That could be 160 workers, 30 sales staff, 10 engineers and 10 managers.

- **What certifications can he provide for product "X"?**

  Know the certifications that you need for your product. If a supplier has no idea about FCC, CE, RoHS, ERP, GS or other certifications of a chemical or other nature, you can probably leave the booth right away. If he is aware of the certifications and

264

requirements but hasn't applied them to all his products it's not an eliminating criteria, but make sure to ask if he is willing to apply for the certifications after order-placement.

- **Who are his main customers?**

Do you know the customers he is talking about? Do they have a certain reputation in your country that would make you feel comfortable working with him? If he is working with customers that you know, it should be a good sign of his competence.

- **Mention a few of your competitors or bigger clients**

Drop a few names of the bigger competitors or clients of yours. If he knows them it's a good sign. If not, it is very unlikely that they are doing overseas business and perhaps aren't even interested in your business, knowing that your requirements are too high or "too much work" for him.

- **What is his main market?**

If he operates already within or near your country it is also likely that he can fulfill your requirements. It's usually a good sign if he works for countries like the UK, Germany, Switzerland, Sweden, the United States, Canada and other first world countries. It means that his factory is able to pass audits, tests and certifications needed for these countries.

- **What is the factory standard?**

Remember that good factories are also easy to spot if they have a certain quality management System (QMS) such as ISO 9001, BSCI and so on.

- **What is the MOQ?**

Can he actually provide the low or high MOQ that you need? Is he willing to produce a first order based on a very small quantity or does he have the capacity for large volumes?

- **What is the rough price of this item based on X quantity?**

Most suppliers will give you a very rough figure for the product they are exhibiting. These can be vague as often these are "blank" prices that do not include any certification, licenses, etc. But it is necessary to ask for prices (and write them down in your notebook) for your follow up. You can also use my "rule of thumb" to add on 20-30% on top of the supplier's price to calculate if the price is competitive.

- **What certification is included in his price?**

Does the product currently fulfill your minimum requirements for certifications or standards? If not, is he willing to apply for certifications after order placement? Is he aware of the different certifications that you need or do you get the feeling he doesn't know what you are talking about?

- **Ask if he can provide samples after the exhibition**

If you would like to have a sample after you come back home ask him if he is willing to send samples. Most likely he will agree but make sure you remind him once you are back home to send you the sample. Some suppliers will actually sell or give you a sample right on the booth if you ask for it. It is actually not allowed but if there is a sample I would need right away because it's that good and I want to show it to customers back home, I will ask anyway.

- **Ask for payment terms**

  Are his payment terms a K.O. criteria? Make sure he agrees to your payment terms and doesn't insist on 100% payment upfront.

- **Ask for his top-selling items and who his customers are**

  Sometimes you may not have time to look at all products so you might miss the best selling items. Ask him either to show you his best selling items or send you a quote later for his top-sellers. Make a note that you are expecting his prices and offers later.

If I get the feeling after 1 or 2 questions that a supplier has no idea what I am talking or asking about, I politely end the conversation and leave the booth. There is no use in screening a supplier with all questions when I already know he is not interested or can't fulfill my requirements.

After all, I need to scan the entire exhibition and I can't waste my time with suppliers that are ignorant or need a basic education on my market's/customer's requirements. You will develop a gut feeling pretty soon if it is worth it to speak to a supplier longer or if you should leave the booth right away.

How to spot good and bad factories

You can easily spot the good from the bad factories by asking all the questions above. If his customer base is small or his answers are weary you should stay away. If you still would like to continue with this supplier make sure that you follow up on all of your requirements in writing by email.

Know your goals

Remember you don't have all day. I usually try to finish an exhibition within 1 day (except the Canton Fair). But this is also because I know how to spot the good from the bad ones and know which questions to ask. As a first timer I recommend you take some more time but don't try to spend more than 20 minutes per booth with each supplier.

If you spot some item that really catches your attention and you would like to discuss further steps with the supplier right away, take your time.

It is likely you will have 2-3 meetings that can take an hour.

Price preparation

You will likely be looking for a category of a product so you should prepare yourself with some basic prices that you have received from suppliers beforehand. Knowing your prices is essential before going to an exhibition.

If you are looking at new products and are not aware of prices try my "rule of thumb" calculation of 30%, adding this to your margin and calculating your selling price. You will quickly figure out if the price the supplier gave you at the booth is realistic or not.

Prioritizing

Some exhibitions are enormous in size. Grab a map at the entrance or the information counter of the exhibition and take a moment to study the areas of interest. You can also look online prior to going to the exhibitions at which hall or category is where to save some time.

Once it is clear where your suppliers are situated, start there. Go through each hall in an organized way and prioritize the halls by importance.

Once you completed all the halls you wanted to see you could go to the halls that were initially of the least interest to your business. You may find some ideas on other products in less interesting halls too.

HOTELS DURING THE EXHIBTIONS:

Many hotels will provide a free shuttle bus to exhibitions. Check with the hotel staff to see if this service is provided.

Book hotels now if you haven't booked them yet! Hotels during exhibitions can get very expensive. The sooner you book the better.

I usually won't stay too far from the exhibition area, as I don't want to waste time. Unfortunately that carries a price tag.

If your budget doesn't allow this, find a hotel near a subway (MTR).

Whatever you do, don't take a taxi TO and FROM the exhibition. Take the subway or free shuttle buses provided by your hotel. At the Canton Fair, for example, it is impossible to get taxis at night. You can take a taxi in the morning TO the fair; that should be ok.

Once you are at the exhibition, get a map; you should be able to get them anywhere.

CHAPTER 12
AT THE FACTORY

It makes sense to pre-arrange meetings before your trip with existing and potential suppliers.

Simply follow the guidelines on preparation and instruct your supplier of your visit.

Sometimes during exhibitions I will meet a good supplier there and I will try to arrange a factory tour right after the exhibition. Most times the exhibiting suppliers will still have staff at the factories so that you can visit even while they are exhibiting.

Once you have arranged a meeting with the supplier and you arrive at the factory a representative will usually greet you and bring you to the **meeting room.**

Once you sit down you should give a **brief introduction** about yourself and your company. This shouldn't take longer than 10 minutes.

You should usually have a brief meeting in their showroom first to exchange pleasantries and then take a factory tour followed by a detailed sit-down in the showroom to discuss products and other details.

Once you arrive at the factory ask **what time the factory will have lunch break**. Most factories will have lunch break around 11.30am-1pm. So make sure you arrive well before 11.30am or take a factory tour first before the sit-down.

Otherwise, you might be touring an empty factory after the first sit-down. And you **definitely came to see production** in the factory and to see how things are assembled or made.

Suppliers sometimes forget that step and it happened to me before, that I arrived at the factory, sat down for a while and discussed things only to realize workers had gone for lunch once our meeting was finished.

You can **also politely ask about lunch arrangements**. I prefer the supplier to order in some fast food that would typically arrive after the production visit. If you have time for a lunch with the supplier you can discuss it now.

If you have time to discuss all details before the production visit, here are some **general meeting guidelines**:

- **Have your pre-printed checklist ready on which you can take notes. It could look something like this:**

Vendor Profile Report

COMPANY PROFILE

Company Name:	
Address:	Street:
	City: Country: China
Phone/Fax/E-mail	Phone: Fax:
	E-Mail:
Contact Person:	Position:

Banker's Name:	A/C No.:
Address:	Street: Phone:
	City: Country: Fax:
	SWIFT: Regional no. of the bank: IBAN-Code:

Year of Establishment:	Number of Employees: Office: Factory:
Ownership:	☐ Private ☐ Public ☐ State
	☐ Joint Venture ☐ Belongs to Group ☐ Other:
Business Category:	☐ Maker ☐ Trader ☐ Trader/Maker ☐ Corporation
Main Articles:	

Turnover / Year: (Mio USD)	Domestic:
	Export:

Production capacity (in piece)	Per Day	Per Month	Per Year

Customers : (Export)	Article	Main Customer	Country	Turnover Last Year
1				
2				
3				
4				
...				

Quota(s): (if applicable)	Country	Category	Quota	QTY Holding
1				
2				
...				

Trade Fair Participation:	☐ Yes ☐ No
	Main Expos / Cities:
Showroom:	☐ Yes Location:
Certificates:	☐ ISO 9... ☐ GS ☐ Others:

Business Terms

Payment Terms:	
Min. Order Quantity:	
Delivery Lead Time:	Initial Order: Repeat Order:

272

FACTORY PROFILE

Factory Name:				
Location:	Street:			
	City:		Country:	
Phone/Fax/E-mail	Phone:		Fax:	E-Mail:
Contact Person:			Position:	
Distance from...(hrs)	Airport:		Station:	Hotel:

Production machine with quantity :	

Production Sub-contracting	☐ Yes

Own Brand(s):	☐ Yes	☐ No
	Names:	

C/O of Raw Material, Components	Country	Delivery Time

Size (sqm):	Property:		Warehouse:		Production site:
Personnel Structure: (Staff Headcount)	Admin:	Production:		R & D:	QA:

Quality Management System	☐ Yes	☐ Certified	☐ No	☐ Planned in _____ (year)

(I have these templates within my ImportDojo Masterclass)

- Ask for a brief introduction of the supplier and his factory. Most suppliers will have a company PowerPoint presentation.
- Ask about his business and turnover figures
- Does he have insights on upcoming trends to share with you?
- What are his goals in the near future in terms of product and customer development?
- Is he investing in new technologies or looking into other product categories that could be interesting for you?
- What is he doing to battle raw material and labor cost increases?

273

- **State the purpose of your visit and go through it step by step.**

You can basically also ask **all the questions from the exhibition chapter.** They pretty much apply for the factory as well and can help you to filter things.

Usually a factory has a **showroom** with the supplier's products. Follow these steps:

- **Walk through the showroom with the supplier and let him give you details and explanations of his products.**
- **Ask for his best sellers and unique products.**
- **Make sure that he or his assistant takes notes and will follow up after your meeting.**
- **Take photos and notes yourself of the products you are interested in.**

Once you have finished your showroom tour and general meeting it is time to **visit the product line.**

When I walk through the factory I look at the following things and ask about them:

- **Production lines**

  How many are there? Is the production busy or empty? If empty, ask for the reasons. Is there a quality control at the end of each production line to assure the product's functionality?

- **Quality control**

  Usually factories have a separate quality control room with some inspectors and engineers, testing their current or new products. In there they should also have all the documentation and certifications of their products. Ask to see a certificate of a certain product. Even if you don't understand it, take a look.

- **Machinery**

What machinery do they use? Is it old or new machinery? Ask if he has invested in new machinery lately or if he is planning to.

- **Work shop**

Do they have their own tooling shop or are they outsourcing all tooling and tooling maintenance? It is usually a good sign if they have a work/tooling shop because this way they control their tooling and maintenance of machinery more efficiently.

- **Warehouse**

Is the warehouse in a mess or rather organized? What other customers packagings and outgoing shipments can you see? Is he selling to your competitors or perhaps to a new potential client for you?

- **R&D department**

How much attention goes into their R&D (research and development)? Is he simply copying other supplier's products or are they actually investing in new products and designs? A good R&D department can be crucial to product development, hence feeding you new product ideas.

- **Incoming material**

Is the incoming material documented and checked once it arrives? Do they keep records of all their raw-material suppliers?

275

- **Competitor's production**

  Keep an eye out during the whole production visit for other customer's or competitor's production. There are usually a lot of cartons and packaging lying around that could give you your next potential customer or product idea. It is also an indication of whether he is competent enough to deal with the market you are operating in.

I also take samples **off the actual production line**. Don't be shy, take an item off the production line, inspect it, bend it and ask anything that you want to know.

After the production visit it is up to you to go into the meeting room again and discuss anything that is still on your mind.

I always **repeat the discussed topics** and make sure the supplier has understood what I need him to do now. We will **set a deadline** on when prices, samples or material will be sent and what he needs from me to complete this task.

I also set myself a reminder for that deadline to remind him if no feedback has been received.

It is also a good opportunity to **discuss any future bonus agreements, claims or compensations** of previous orders. Take a look at Chapter 6 of Part 1 of this course (advanced negotiations).

Once you finish the meeting and factory tour ask your supplier to drive you to your next appointment or back to the hotel. **Remember to pre-inform** your supplier before the meeting of your travel arrangements.

If he invites you for dinner and you have time I recommend you to join him. It is most likely a Chinese restaurant or the restaurant of your hotel that he will invite you to. I enjoy these dinners as the supplier loosens up a lot and probably gives away some industry secrets or information about what my competitor is up to.

CHAPTER 13
AFTER THE TRIP

You have to follow up on what you and the supplier discussed.

Once I get back home or to my office I start following up immediately. I don't wait around for the supplier to send me the offers or the discussed material.

I want to get started right away because I have other tasks that need my attention, especially since I have been away on a trip. Often times I do it the same day after the meeting on my way to the hotel or at the hotel.

So if a supplier hasn't sent me the follow up material yet I will drop him an email that could look like this:

> *Dear....,*
>
> *Many thanks again for your time during our meeting at the (factory/exhibition/hotel, etc.).*
>
> *I would like to re-cap the discussed points and need your earliest feedback:*
>
> *Quotes for...*
> *Pictures of the discussed product*
> *Etc.*
>
> *Please send me ..... At your earliest convenience so that I can follow up also from my side.*

If you do have any questions please don't hesitate to contact me.

Thanks and best regards,

Manuel

Look at your notes from the trip and remind the supplier of missed topics if necessary.

CHAPTER 14
SUMMARY & WAYS TO SAVE YOU MONEY

You see there are a few procedures and guidelines that you can follow to make your trip and import from China a successful one.

In time you will get a good feeling for each step of the import process and it will come naturally.

When I started over 10 years ago I was at the same stage that you are now (or probably behind you). I hope that my experience written down in this course and the *Import Bible* will help you along the way to build your import empire.

To sum up some of the tips and tricks in previous chapters (including the *Import Bible*) I want to outline them here again:

1) Sample agreements

Samples can cost you a lot of money over time. Most factories will charge you for samples. Even if you are a big retailer, factories will likely ask you to pay.

You can certainly ask to waive the sample costs. On the other hand you can also ask the supplier to pay the sample costs and say that you'll take care of the freight costs. This way you will share 50/50 of the costs.

Try to avoid paying for samples all the time by making agreements that once you place an order the sample costs will be deducted from the invoice.

Also, you should ask your supplier for free samples in the future after you have established business with him.

To avoid high freight costs ask your supplier to send samples with his courier service. Tell him that you prepay sample and freight costs and they should use their courier account. They probably have better courier rates.

NEVER give away your courier express number (if you do have one). I have had suppliers use my account for other customers.

2) Inspection & re-inspection agreements

If you have a "failed" inspection result you should do a re-inspection, depending on the seriousness of the found problems. If you have scratches, dents or minor mistakes on a few inspected items you can probably ask your supplier to re-work the goods and send you a Letter of Guarantee.

However, if there are more serious mistakes you should have a re-inspection and this time the supplier should pay for it. This should be agreed on before placing an order to a supplier. Simply include this purchasing term in your official order form and have him sign it.

3) Bonus agreements

Once you have established business with your supplier you should have bonus agreements in place that guarantee you money back at the end of the year. Even if it's not much, it could cover traveling costs for your next trip to China or your next holiday or gadget.

4) Travel for free within China

Remember to arrange a car from each supplier to pick you up and bring you to your next appointment. Most suppliers will provide you with a mini-van that has a lot of space and you can work on your emails while travelling to your next appointment or take a nap after a stressful day.

5) Calculate your costs

Calculating your costs appropriately makes or breaks your import. Remember this! Make sure you take all costs into account, such as taxes, duties, licenses, freight costs or associated fees. Keep track of each cost on a sheet and calculate your expected profit.

6) Hire inspection companies

You don't want to open ordered goods back home and find that either the wrong product has arrived or that there are major problems with quality. Inspections are affordable and should be done for larger orders. If you have small orders through drop shipping or just a few pieces you can skip this part.

7) Product to market fit

Do your research and be diligent. Make sure your new product isn't out there already and has a product-to-market-fit.

8) Shopping lists

Work with a research list (or shopping list as I call it) to track your ideas and new products. Send them to your (trusted) suppliers and ask them to give you quotes for the same or similar items. Copy links in your list so that you can make reference again at a later stage. Look through your lists once in a while and get inspired.

9) Proper documentation & administration

It is vital to have proper documentation and administration. You may need to refer back to an email or letter from a supplier months or years later that stated something that you relied on. You will also want to keep a proper organization for your own sake.

10) Negotiate re-orders

Make sure to ask for a discount on your next order, even if your quantity is smaller this time. You have power in hand when you have your official order ready to send. Suppliers are likely to give you a discount on your next re-order.

11) The 6-step import process

Follow this process for each product life cycle. It applies every time. Each product idea you have should go through at least a rough check with each step to make sure your article will sell and not end up in your warehouse.

12) Aliexpress vs. Alibaba negotiation tip

Here's a pretty nice tip I've discovered and use whenever I can. I always check aliexpress first for what I'm looking for. I then contact the supplier and ask for the amount that I want to purchase (usually a lot more than the amount they are selling on aliexpress) and if they can give me a quote for a bulk discount.

Usually they respond pretty quickly and we come to a price. I then place an order via aliexpress for the amount of that product that I want (but don't pay for it yet) and have them change the price to the price that we agreed on. I then pay for the items and now I have the aliexpress security blanket set for me so I can get refunded if they scam me.

13) Let Global Sources or Alibaba source for you

They provide sourcing services, you just tell them what you are looking for and then they source from well-known and respected suppliers, all FOR FREE.

14) Hire an inspection service and decide on the AQL level yourself

You will want a minimum of 5% to be inspected when you do a shipment inspection. You hire them, send them a sample or tell them what there is to be inspected. Then you ask your factory for a date when 80% of the goods will be finished. This is the date you give your inspection company to go and inspect.

On the day after the inspection you will get a report on which you base your decision of releasing the shipment or not. If there is re-work to be done don't worry, the supplier will have to do it, otherwise he won't get his 70% payment (since you should never pay 100% up front).

PART 4
SUPPORT

If anything in this eBook hasn't been covered you may contact me directly at: mail@importdojo.com

I will try to answer all questions that you may have within a reasonable amount of time.

For other topics on import or if you would like to use us as your sourcing agent please contact me at the above email or through our website:
http://www.manuelbecvar.com OR www.importdojo.com

Remember to sign up for my FREE Facebook groups:

Facebook group for making money online and entrepreneurial things:
https://www.facebook.com/groups/504810863347354/

Facebook group for importing from China and Amazon FBA:
https://www.facebook.com/groups/1585493201714528/?ref=br_rs

Printed in Great Britain
by Amazon